Donald's
Book
of
Golf
Lists

A.K.A.

HOLE-IN-ONE PAIR of PANTS

Congratulations!
Enjoy.
Donald Miller

Donald's Book of Golf Lists

A.K.A.

HOLE-IN-ONE PAIR of PANTS

by Donald C. Miller

RoseDog✿Books

PITTSBURGH, PENNSYLVANIA 15222

ISBN # 0-8059-9566-8
Printed in the United States of America

First Printing

For additional information or to order additional books,
please write:
RoseDog Publishing
701 Smithfield Street
Pittsburgh, Pennsylvania 15222
U.S.A.
1-800-834-1803
Or visit our web site and on-line bookstore at
www.rosedogbookstore.com

"Our everyday life is an interruption that intrudes on our golf games."

—-Dr. Richard Coop

Table of Contents

Forewords xi

I.   Introduction 1

II.   Palmer Lists 5

III.   Instructional Lists 9

IV.   Handy Reference Lists 28

V.   DeBunkering Golf's Myths 82

VI.   Personal Lists 104

VII.   Incomplete Lists 109

VIII.   The Final Elbow 127

Afterword 133

Bibliography 135

Appendix 139

Consumer Alert:

Hole-In-One Pair of Pants

is the only golf publication

guaranteed to be

RADON Free

and

Y3K Compliant.

Donald's Book of Golf Lists

has earned

the Practical Golf Consortium's

Seal of Approval

Foreword I

By Frank Maitz

When Donald asked me to write the Foreword for his book, I was flattered, honored, and admittedly, overwhelmed. Not being a professional writer, how could I **EVER** do justice to his labor of love, and more importantly, to Donald? So I am giving him the authority to ask Tom Clancy, or even Mark Twain's great-great-great grandniece Shania to open this book.

I must admit my enthusiasm waned as I watched the pages print from the download he sent me. "How dare he?" I yelped. "Not another book of lists!! Who needs another **#!?%** list??" At least this was my initial thought as I opened Donald's manuscript sometime in December of 1999. You see, everyone was publishing some stupid list to mark the end of the 20th Century. Even the world of golf felt obliged to provide a seemingly endless supply of meaningless lists. I saw no lists, however, giving any compelling reasons why "the masses of men" couldn't hold their water and wait until the following year for the real start of the 3rd millennium. Thoreau would not be surprised by modern man's haste. So I thank Donald for his patience with me. It is only fitting that his literary masterpiece signals the start of the next 1000 years.

Donald's book of lists is unique; to say the least, as is Donald. I can only compare Donald's approach to golf (and life) to that of Van Gogh's approach to painting, thoroughly

1. Original,
2. Insightful,
3. Thought-provoking,
4. Passionate.

Oops, sorry. You'll be seeing enough lists shortly.

Just as Vincent threw away his brushes and smeared paint on his canvasses with his bare hands, Donald has punched his monitor and assaulted his keyboard with fist-a-flying! Donald would NEVER make a list of the top 10 money winners of all time. Meaningless. NEVER a list of the longest drivers, or the best putters, or the lowest scores. We all know golf is a far more cerebral game than that.

Donald brings to his lists guaranteed smiles, not just statistics. He will take you on a journey to the Azalea Open (what Open?). He will instruct you on how to make a Hole in 9. Donald challenges the ancient tenets of golf instruction by "Debunkering Golf's Myths." Donald will also introduce you to the best sources to discover golf history, instruction and tradition. It is the only golf reference book you'll ever need.

My friend Donald has written this book. Donald is not a professional golfer. His chances (and mine) of ever shooting par or playing Augusta National are, well, beyond remote. This book is purely his labor of love. After you read it, you will agree. Enjoyable at every turn, the ironic ending will smack you right in your gullible kisser.

You won't have to live with that empty feeling of wanting more for long. Donald is hotly working on his follow-up, "The Book of Baseball Lists." I can't wait to find out why Mickey Mantle and Willie Mays are NOT on his all-time best team list. Or who can wait for his all left-handed team, or all Lithuanian, or all under 5' 5", or…

Foreword II

By Ronald Marple

When Donald Miller called and asked me to contribute a foreword for *Donald's Book of Golf Lists*, my initial response was: "Who?….Why?" After a lengthy and wearisome conversation, I conjured a vague recollection of a nettlesome pro-am partner in an obscure charity event. I reluctantly agreed to peruse a copy of Mr. Miller's literary abortion.

It came as no surprise to discover that his mediocre golfing talent was on par with his writing ability. It was also clearly discernible that no self-respecting human being would ever read this drivel. In the unlikely event that an unsuspecting reader is accidentally exposed to this unmeritorious malaise, I felt compelled to forewarn the unfortunate victim: the Surgeon General has determined that prolonged exposure to *Hole-In-One Pair of Pants* will result in a severely brain damaged condition requiring lobotomy. Side effects may include halitosis and erectile dysfunction.

I also felt obligated to expose the absurdity of Mr. Miller's discourse. Mimicking his repulsive and undisciplined style of list generation, I _fabricated a list that challenges the integrity of lists in *Donald's Book of Golf Lists*

Beverage Service Menu from Southwest Airlines Golf Vacation Package

1. COCKTAILS/$4.00
    -Dewars Scotch
    -Smirnoff Vodka
    -Jack Daniels
    -Wild Turkey
    -Jim Beam
    -Crown Royal
    -Tanqueray Gin

-Bacardi Rum
-Bailey's Irish Cream
-Bacardi Limon
-Jose Cuervo
-Courvoisier VSOP
-Malibu Caribbean Coconut Rum
-Finlandia Vodka

2. WINE/$3.00
-Heritage Chardonnay
-Heritage White Zinfandel
-Heritage Merlot

3. BEER/$3.00
-Coors Light
-Budweiser
-Bud Light
-Miller Lite
-Heineken

4. NON-ALCOHOLIC
-Coca-Cola classic
-Diet Coke
-Sprite
-Diet Sprite
-Cool from Nestea
-Dr Pepper
-Diet Dr Pepper
-Ginger Ale
-Tonic Water
-Bloody Mary Mix
-Orange Juice
-Grapefruit Juice
-Apple Juice
-Tomato Juice
-Cranberry Apple Juice
-Carbonated Water
-Non-Carbonated Spring Water
-Coffee
-Decaf Singles
-Tea

-Hot Cocoa

—-from *Spirit*

I would be remiss in recommending a golf vacation package if the airline's beverage menu does not include Killian's Irish Red and Yoo-hoo.

The fabricated example reflects Mr. Miller's lack of literary couth. Thus it is my moral and civic duty to deter the proletariat from the social and ethical disgrace implicit in owning and reading this book.

Ronald Marple's Advice re
<u>Hole-In-One Pair of Golf Lists</u>

1. Avoid intellectual exposure to this book.
2. Do not put this book on your shopping LIST.
3. Avert your eyes if you see this book in the bookstore.
4. Close cover before striking.
5. WALK or DON'T WALK.
6. *#*?*!!

I. Introduction

"When someone offers you advice,
listen politely and then say,
'That's exactly what my pro suggested
and just what I'm working on.'
Then go back to what you were doing
and concentrate that much harder."

—-Jim Flick

One more book about golf...that's all it is. *Hole-In-One Pair of Pants* is just one more book about golf.

1. It is not an instructional panacea.
2. It is not an ostentatious technical manual.
3. It is not an authoritative encyclopedia.
4. It is not a comprehensive and unabridged examination of golf's history.
5. It is not an attempt to rationalize our irresistible attraction to the game of golf.
6. It is not an endeavor as William Hallberg cogently declares "...to dissect the vast metaphor of golf...to probe the conundrums of the greenest sport known to man."
7. It is definitely not a definitive book of lists.

Welcome to *Donald's Book of Golf Lists*, an uncomplicated book of simple lists. I'm Donald Miller and I'm your peripatetic host for 233,771.55 metric pages of trivia, minutiae, esoterica and other unimportant matters lacking substance and depth.

All seriousness aside, why did I write one more book about golf? In addition to the universal motives: self-affirmation, monetary reward and a congenital pre-occupation with the subject of golf (A panel of Harvard researchers possesses verifiable medical documentation confirming that I performed multiple practice swings in the womb), twelve disparate (and totally unrelated) reasons come to mind.

1. Lists have universal appeal. How else can we account for the success of *The Book of Lists* by David Wallechinsky and Irving Wallace...and what about the perennial popularity of David Letterman's Top Ten lists? I'm sure it's on every anthropologist's list of distinguishing human characteristics: Homo sapiens are listmakers.

2. Golf is a captivating and enchanting topic. In his introduction to *Bobby Jones on Golf*, Mr. Jones wrote of golf's eternal appeal: "Golf is an inexhaustible subject. I cannot imagine that anyone might ever write every word that needs to be written about the golf swing." Furthermore, as Andrew Shanley commented in *Fathers, Sons & Golf*, "Golfers require only modest expectation of insight, because they yearn for it so." Or more succinctly, consider this paraphrase of Congressman Morris Udall's comment at the Democratic Convention of 1988: even if everything on the subject of golf has been written, not everyone has written it.

3. If Gary McCord can write a book, anyone can write a book.

4. Yet another paraphrase of an observation by Ken Blanchard in *Playing the Great Game of Golf*: the worst a book about golf can be is great.

5. This dissertation has provided me the opportunity to consolidate and amalgamate all of the acquired knowledge (books, articles, individual observations and opinions) that has influenced my golfing persona.

6. An abundant number of erudite and eloquent books have been written on the subject of golf. My unrefined observations and opinions will provide a necessary counterpoint to all of that scholarship.

7. Popular acceptance of this literary opus presents the possibility—albeit remote—-that the author attains minor celebrity status, e.g. a guest appearance on MTV or an invitation to compete in the pro-am segment of an LPGA tournament.

8. Inasmuch as lists can be readily excerpted, the fluff contained in this book could receive extensive exposure as mass market filler, i.e. the

literary equivalent of kitty litter.

9. Isn't Oprah about due to endorse a provocative and appealing golf book from a promising unknown author? Hey, girlfriend. Here you go.

10. In order that future generations may continue to enjoy the great game of golf, all of the visionary information contained within these pages is Y3K compliant. For a nominal fee, I will provide the reader with a written guarantee that every word in *Donald's Book of Golf Lists* will remain meaningful and provocative beyond the year 3000.

11. It would be sinful to waste the extraordinary literary talent in the Miller gene pool. My son Max affirmed the depth of this talent when he composed the following poem at the age of seven:

Flying Squirrel

Flys and glides through the day air
Leaving its home and going some where.
Yipping and yapping as it glides along
Ignoring the forests lovely song.
No it won't stop till it finds what it needs
Gliding through the very strong breeze.
Shivering when it glides through the snow
Quivering as it sees plants grow.
Up and down zipping around
Incisors gnaw at nuts aloud.
Ripping its wings is very bad
Ripping its wings is very sad.
Evolution is its name.
Learning about him is my game.

12. Finally, this book is my platform for proposing a "new" instructional paradigm based on the synthesis of observation and participation.

Golf instructor Sandy Jaskol compares golf to an "experimental" walk in the park. The golfer experiments until he performs the appropriate action. When the golfer does something "wrong," it's not really wrong, it's just inappropriate for what he intended to do. Since you can't do anything wrong, Jaskol asserts that the pressure is off. She recommends that golfers should relax and enjoy their "experimental" walk in the park. For me, *Hole-One-In One Pair of Pants* is an experimental excursion into the realm of writing. If I do something "wrong," it's not really wrong, it's just inappropriate for what I intended to write. The pressure is off. I'm relaxed and ready to enjoy my experimental journey through the land of the written word.

Ultimately, my fate rests with you, the jury. I have attempted to produce a work that is outlandish, opinionated and obtuse. When you judge my efforts, please consider the following wisdom from Meatloaf: "Two out of three ain't bad!"

I want to thank the following people for their unflagging devotion, encouragement, intellectual stimulation and moral support: my wife, Susy; my sons, Max and Gus; Kellen; "Uncle" Frank; Bullwinkle T. Moose; the Kinks.

I also need to say a special thank you to my close friend Ronald Marple for the gracious and complimentary message in the Foreword. Mr. Marple truly exemplifies the generosity of the human spirit. With a friend like Ron, who needs jockey shorts?

Happy Golfing!

II. Palmer Lists

"No book about golf in the modern era should begin with anyone other than Arnold Palmer."
—-Glen Waggoner

Palmers
1. **Arnold Palmer**; 1954 U.S. Amateur Champion and winner of a "few" professional tournaments including 1961 Baton Rouge Open, 1963 Pensacola Open and 1964 Oklahoma City Open.
2. **Sandra Palmer**; 1972 Titleholders Champion, 1975 Colgate Dinah Shore Winner's Circle Champion, 1975 U.S. Women's Open Champion, 1975 LPGA Player of the Year and winner of 21 LPGA tournaments.
3. **Johnny Palmer**; winner of 7 PGA tournaments including the 1947 Western Open and the 1952 Canadian Open.
4. **Milfred J. "Deacon" Palmer**; patriarch.
5. **Raymond Palmer**; 1967 USGA Senior Amateur Champion, 1973 North and South Seniors Champion, 1974 American Seniors Match Play Champion.
6. **Winnie Palmer**; the King's spouse extraordinaire.
7. **Betsy Palmer**; panelist on *I've Got A Secret* starring Garry Moore.

Boldness and Trouble
1. I suppose there's a place to play it safe, but it's not on the golf course.
2. When I take a shot that seems bold, it never occurs to me that I might miss it. And when I do, I'm surprised as hell.
3. don't look on trouble as a gamble. I just look on it as a harder shot.
4. Why hit a conservative shot? When you miss it, you're in just as much trouble as when you miss a bold one.

5. You've got to learn to live with trouble, and you've got to learn how to get out of it. You tell yourself there's nothing here you haven't faced before; and if you've done it once, you can do it again.
6. Trouble is bad to get into but fun to get out of. If you can see the ball, you can probably hit it; and if you can hit it, you can move it; and if you can move it, you might be able to knock it into the hole.

—from *Arnold Palmer: A Personal Journey* by Thomas Hauser

In an April 1992 *Golf Digest* interview, former Masters and PGA Champion Jackie Burke echoes a comparable viewpoint on boldness: "Golf is not for conservative people. Golf is a risky game. Every shot has an element of risk and too many people try to play the game riskless." If a player isn't willing to risk in golf, he isn't *in* the game. If he is judged against these guidelines, Mr. Palmer is always *in* the game.

Putting Creed
1. Hold the putter any way you like.
2. Use any kind of stance you want.
3. If it works, it's right. It's an instinctive function.
4. The way to hole a putt is not to try. Just do it.
5. There's only one mechanical secret: your body has to be totally motionless while you stroke the ball.
6. Putt past the pin. Give it a chance.
7. The correct number of putts that should be taken by a good golfer is one per green.

—Palmer/Hauser

1st Ten Professional Victories
1. Canadian Open, 1955
2. Panama Open, 1956
3. Columbia Open, 1956
4. Insurance City Open, 1956
5. Eastern Open, 1956
6. Houston Open, 1957
7. Azaela Open, 1957
8. Rubber City Open, 1957
9. San Diego Open, 1957
10. St. Petersburg Open, 1958

Mr. Palmer won his first professional major, The Masters, in 1958. In the four year period, 1960—1963, he collected thirty titles including five major championships. His total dominance of the professional tour during these years is without precedence in the annals of golf.

Major Championship Victories

1.	U. S. Amateur	1954
2.	The Masters	1958
3.	The Masters &	
4.	U.S. Open	1960
5.	British Open	1961
6.	The Masters &	
7.	British Open	1962
8.	The Masters	1964

Senior Tour Titles

1. Canadian PGA Championship, 1980
2. PGA Seniors Championship, 1980
3. US Senior Open, 1981
4. Marlboro Classic, 1982
5. Denver Post Champions, 1982
6. Boca Grove Senior Classic, 1983
7. PGA Seniors Championship, 1984
8. Doug Sanders Celebrity Pro-Am, 1984
9. Senior TPC, 1984
10. Quadel Senior Classic, 1984
11. Senior TPC, 1985
12. Unionmutual Classic, 1986
13. Crestar Classic, 1988
14.

As of this writing our legendary hero has not recorded a victory on the Senior PGA Tour in more than ten years. Nevertheless a fervent hope burns in the loyal hearts of his ubiquitous army that the beloved "General" will wage yet another winning campaign. It would be the most glorious triumph in the history of the game.

Past Leading Money Winners/Selected Years

1935 - Johnny Revolta $ 9,543

1940 - Ben Hogan	10,655
1945 - Byron Nelson	63,335
1950 - Sam Snead	35,758
1955 - Julius Boros	63,121
1956 - Ted Kroll	72,835
1957 - Dick Mayer	65,835
1958 - Arnold Palmer	42,607
1959 - Art Wall	53,167
1960 - Arnold Palmer	75,262
1961 - Gary Player	64,540
1962 - Arnold Palmer	81,448
1963 - Arnold Palmer	128,230
1964 - Jack Nicklaus	113,284
1965 - Jack Nicklaus	140,752
1966 - Billy Casper	121,944
1967 - Jack Nicklaus	188.988
1968 - Billy Casper	205,168
1969 - Frank Beard	175,223
1970 - Lee Trevino	157,037
1975 - Jack Nicklaus	298,149
1980 - Tom Watson	530,808
1985 - Curtis Strange	542,321
1990 – Greg Norman	1,165,477
1995 – Greg Norman	1,654,959
2000 – Tiger Woods	9,188,321

The PGA Tour honors the leading money winner of the year with the Arnold Palmer Award. As a genuine golfing icon, Palmer enjoys immunity from viruses, trojans, varmints and infidels.

Happy Golfing!

III. Instructional Lists

"Golf technique is a smorgasbord of possibilities
that can be sampled, not a religion to be obeyed."
—-Jon Markovy

"The game is deceptively simple—-
put the ball in the hole.
But it reveals itself
at a stately pace,
one secret at a time,
to even the most ardent practitioner."
—-Mark Frost

"The trick is to amalgamate
the clichés into a
comprehensible truth.
The trick is to separate subtext
from pretext."
—-William Hallberg

Chuck Hogan says: "There is always a better golfer inside struggling to get out!" It is difficult to disagree with Mr. Hogan's conclusion about the better golfer inside of each of us, but the observation by venerable columnist Jim Murray that golf is an overtaught and underlearned endeavor is equally undeniable. The key is to stimulate learning while not overburdening the pupil with excessive teaching.

The following instructional lists represent a broad historical cross section of golf tips and advice: Armour, Vardon, Hogan, Nelson, Player, Watson, Thomson, Casper, Flick, Knudson, Waggoner and more. Since there is no universal framework in the area of golf instruction, it is highly probable that one of the lists contains a revelation—-a statement that makes you say "Aha!"——regardless of your skill level and proficiency. If you are a genuine golf addict, the possibility of that single enlightening insight is sufficient justification for reading this book.

As you will see repeatedly throughout this book, I am not a proponent of structured practice. It is not realistic to learn a movement on the practice tee since you will only have to re-learn that movement on the course. In spite of your best efforts and complete dedication to practice, you will never simulate the playing conditions unique to the course. What is the right way to hit a golf ball? It depends on who's holding the club. The golf course is the laboratory in which you must discover "your method" by experimentation and observation.

Intelligent judgment and simplicity of technique are the foundation of good golf. Regular play is the best method for developing judgment and refining technique. If one of the tips or recommendations contained in the subsequent lists fits the common sense guidelines for how **YOU** play the game, you must immediately and unerringly implement it in an actual round of golf. Evaluate your results ("Results? I have gotten a lot of results. I know several thousand things that won't work." ——Thomas Edison) and tailor the tip, if necessary, until you achieve the desired outcome. It could be astounding. Remember: It's up to you; it's YOUR game to learn and enjoy. Contrary to the popular bromide, it is not fruitless to indoctrinate a superannuated canine with innovative maneuvers, or as Uncle Frank would say: "You CAN teach an old dog new tricks."

The Simple Routine of an Orderly Shot

1. Study the shot to be played, particularly in relationship to your capabilities.
2. Select the right club (and tee the ball correctly if it's a tee shot).
3. Take the correct grip.
4. Take the correct stance for the shot to be played.
5. Keep your head steady.
6. See that your left knee points behind the ball on the backswing.
7. Have your wrists broken to the fullest extent at the top of the backswing, without loosening the left hand. The right hand grip is firm, but not tight.
8. Pause at the top of the swing.
9. Don't rush as you start down, but get your right knee in toward the ball.
10. Keep your head steady.
11. Keep your hands ahead of the clubhead by keeping your wrists cocked, and whip your right hand into the shot at the last second.
12. Keep your head steady.

   —from *How to Play Your Best Golf All the Time* by Tommy Armour

Some Hints from Horace Hutchinson

1. "Slow back!"—it is a valuable text to have at heart. Some write it up in their dressing rooms, and read it every morning all the while they shave.
2. All the muscles must be supple; for if any of the motions in the swing are stiff, the rest are certain to be jerky.
3. Always golf your hardest. But yet you must not cultivate this infinite carefulness to the loss of freedom. Do not be so scientific as to lose all dash.
4. Even the worst golfer can play the game perfectly so far as the observance of the rules is concerned; yet even the best often do not. Certainly it would be far more satisfactory if it were universally understood that the game is to be played according to the strict rigor of the rules.
5. Try to remember that a person may be a most indifferent golfer, and yet be a good gentleman, and in some respects worthy of your esteem.
6. Do not use a long club when a short one will answer your purpose better. It is better to be five yards short of a bunker than five yards nearer the hole, in it.
7. Most men will make a better shot with the club they happen to fancy, even though it be palpably the wrong one, than with the right one, which has been put in their hands at your suggestion.
8. The spectator has a perfect right to his opinion. It is only when he begins to act as if it were of value that you are justified in correcting his mistake.
9. Driving is an Art. Iron play is a Science. Putting is an inspiration.

—-from *Hints on Golf* by Horace Hutchinson

The Vardon Method

1. The body should be easy and comfortable at address.
2. The stance should be open, with the rear foot square to the line of play and the leading foot angled toward the target.
3. The ball should be addressed opposite the left heel or, if not there, nearer to the left heel than the right—unless you wish to play a low shot.
4. The arms do not touch the body at address, but neither do they reach.
5. The weight should be divided equally between both feet.
6. It is necessary only to find the correct stance and the shot is certain to be a success.
7. The head should be steady throughout the swing because if it moves, the body goes with it, disrupting the club's path.
8. Avoid straining for too wide a backswing, for if you do, you will likely sway your body.
9. As the backswing proceeds, the right knee holds firm, but does not quite become stiff.

10. Don't lift your heel too much, but let it come comfortably up as you pivot onto the foot in response to your body pivot.
11. There is no pause between the backswing and the downswing; they flow into each other.
12. The downswing is faster than the backswing, but there should be no conscious effort to make it so.
13. At impact the feet should be flat on the ground.
14. At the finish the arms are up, the hands level with the head, the club beyond horizontal, and the body and shoulders face the target.
15. Don't scoop with the iron; thump down on the ball.
16. Good driving is the foundation of a good game.
17. Never throw the clubhead or make a hit with it; swing it all the way.
18. The shorter the swing or the shot, the narrower the stance, the less the foot and body action, and the more the emphasis on the knees. The length of the backswing determines the distance of the less than full shot.
19. The most successful way to play golf is the easiest way.
20. To play well, you must feel tranquil and at peace.

—-from *The Methods of Golf's Masters*:
"Harry Vardon, the Master Mold" by Ken Bowden

Learn to Swing the Modern Way

1. In the modern golf swing, ease and comfort are the watchwords. The best way to swing is the simplest way.
2. In gripping the club, you should feel pressure in the hands but not in the forearms. Make sure your left-hand pressure is dominant.
3. For proper aim and alignment, keep a slightly open stance.
4. The waggle sets the tempo for the whole swing.
5. Begin the takeaway with the left side.
6. Don't overswing on the backswing. A longer backswing will not produce a longer shot.
7. Let your wrists cock gradually and naturally on the backswing.
8. Don't be anxious at the top.
9. Keep your arm speed steady in both directions.
10. On the downswing, the entire left side starts down together, leading the hands and clubhead down, into and through the ball.

—-from *Shape Your Swing the Modern Way* by Byron Nelson

Peter Thomson: Observations and Techniques

1. The best way to play golf is the simplest.
2. The most important facets of golf are careful planning, calm and clear

thinking, and the ordinary logic of common sense. Golf calls for logical observation. Beyond that the big thing is not power but judgment.

3. Golf is at least 50 percent a mental game, and if you recognize that it is the mind that prompts us physically, then you can almost say that golf is entirely a mental effort.

4. One's best golf is played when the body is relaxed and the nerves are quiet

5. You can tell when a golfer is thinking freely. He goes along with his head up and a happy attitude.

6. You think best when you are happiest.

7. You have to like and enjoy what you are doing and where you are doing it. It is a good to idea to make up your mind to like a course you are about to play, to like the people you are playing with, and to enjoy the weather, hot or cold.

8. If you think you are striving to your utmost, then you have nothing in reserve for any adversity that might come your way.

9. Success in golf is 50 percent what you do and 50 percent what other people do. So remember that they may not be doing their 50 percent as well as you are doing yours. Stay calm and alert and recognize your opportunities.

10. Anyone who can walk can play golf. It is a walking game. To be a good golfer you must be a good walker; you must condition your legs.

11. Control of direction pays off better than length. Unbridled power hitting from the tee courts disaster.

12. Plan your round before you tee off. Plan each hole and stick with that plan.

13. Walking with a steady, relaxed rhythm, arms swinging freely, will help your game.

14. Think simply about your swing and you will have a simple, uncomplicated swing. Think simply of drawing the club back, gathering your power, and then hitting the ball precisely forward toward target.

15. A light, tender, sensitive touch is worth a ton of brawn.

—-from *The Methods of Golf's Masters: "A Light, Tender, Sensitive Touch Is Worth A Ton of Brawn"* by Ken Bowden

In "Renaissance Man" (*Golf Magazine*/July 1998) by Charles Happell, Thomson asserts his disdain for golfing academies. The best players are self-made players who rely on their own wits and skill, abstaining formalized instruction. Similarly, Thomson feels that videotape is overrated as a teaching tool. "I always had an image of my swing from within. I did eventually see myself swing on a film, and I was really shocked. I wouldn't watch; it could have destroyed the confidence I had. Until I saw it on video, my swing seemed perfect to me."

Natural Golf

1. You don't play golf to relax. You relax to play golf.
2. The golf swing is a means of connecting a proper starting position to a proper finishing position through weight transfer and rotation.
3. The most effective swing is one that produces consistency and power in balance.
4. Two forms of balance are important in the natural swing motion: static and dynamic balance.
5. The golfer who is balanced in his starting position and his finishing position is in static balance.
6. Static balance is achieved through proper posture, proper weight distribution, proper grip and correct alignment to the target.
7. The golfer who is balanced through the sequence of movements that comprise the swing is in dynamic balance.
8. Dynamic balance is achieved by: putting yourself in static balance, allowing inertia and centrifugal force to take over while transferring your weight and rotating and doing nothing to interfere with your motion (e.g. passive hands).
9. Golf is a target game. The golf swing is a motion toward the target, not toward the ball. Having a clear image of the target in your mind gives you purpose, direction and intent. The more clearly you fix your destination in your mind, the more easily you will reach the objective.
10. Place the left foot outside the left shoulder so that you will be able to finish with your weight on your left foot. A wide stance allows you to finish solidly (in balance) on the left foot.
11. Proper posture is proud posture. We want to stand as tall as we can. By getting the starting position right, you'll have a splendid chance of making a natural swing motion.
12. The purpose of the loading motion is to gather energy. We do so by transferring weight to the right foot while rotating the body around the trunk. There needn't be any urgency in loading. Relax. Transfer your weight. Let the energy accumulate.
13. Passive hands are not inactive hands. It's just that we don't consciously do anything with them.
14. The unloading motion begins when transfer weight from the right foot to the left. The unloading motion is simply a responsive (involuntary) act due to the weight transfer.
15. The finishing position is truly a *form*. You get to the position by allowing the motion to take place. If you're relaxed, your arms will drop naturally to a recessed position in front of your chest.
16. Evaluate your finishing form after each swing. Are you in balance? Are

you at natural height? Are you facing the target? Have you maintained your hand and wrist formation?

17. Every swing you evaluate is an opportunity gained. You learn where your good and bad shots come from.

18. Turning every swing motion into a separate opportunity for learning is the best way to achieve the ideal state of playing one shot at a time.

—from *The Natural Golf Swing* by George Knudson

An eloquent and succinct description of the activity prescribed by Mr. Knudson in numbers 12—14 appears in the section of *The Duffer's Handbook of Golf* entitled "When to Hit":

> "Most golfers have a double fault when it comes to hitting. They hurry the back swing and they hurry the down swing. They are so keen to hit the ball that few of them can wait. The result is they start the down swing before the back swing is finished, and then, applying the punch too quickly, tighten up and check the club head on its way through.
>
> First of all, the back swing must be completed. One thing at a time. When the back swing is finished the downswing must start smoothly, without being rushed. Don't be in a hurry to apply the snap or punch. If you keep the club head increasing its speed on through the ball there is no need of trying to apply any sudden power.
>
> The swing that you take at a cigar stump or dandelion head is usually the right one because you haven't killed all the flexibility in your wrists and arms by hitting too quickly. Attempting to apply extra power simply means tightening the muscular system to the complete destruction of timing, rhythm, smoothness and a cheerful result."

…And Leslie Nielsen: "You're swinging too fast if you start your backswing while the ball is still in the ball washer."

On Golf

1. The good player can sense exactly where the face of the club is pointing at all times. It's a matter of awareness for the instrument. It's a matter of feel.

2. Your hands are the passageways for feel between your body and the club-head.

3. Fingers secure, arms relaxed.
4. To develop feel in your swing, use your imagination.
5. Posture gives your arms room to swing.
6. Low Shot = Low Risk; High Shot = High Risk.
7. Creating the proper trajectory makes more sense than trying to create spin.
8. The ball goes where the sand goes.
9. The best reason I can think of for playing the ball down is not because that's what the Rules of Golf tell you to do. Playing it down helps you learn to adjust to different conditions, to deal with reality, to recover from bad breaks, and to test yourself honestly.
10. Four reasons why a swing works better than a hit:
    - You're more likely to create maximum clubhead speed at the appropriate time, which is at the bottom of the arc.
    - You're less likely to twist the clubface in an effort to create more speed.
    - You're more likely to hit the ball in the center of the clubface.
    - You enlist centrifugal force and gravity as allies in your quest for consistency.

—from *On Golf* by Jim Flick

Key Setup Compensations
You can't retrain your body to make a different swing, but you can make a number of compensations to change the position at which the clubface meets the ball.
1. Grip position
2. Clubface angle
3. Ball position
4. Body alignment
5. Posture
6. Weight distribution

—from *GOLF Magazine*/February 1995

Checkpoints for Women Golfers
1. Clubs with whippy shafts will increase distance for most women.
2. Use a "strong" grip with both hands turned to the right on the club.
3. Consider a 10-finger grip.
4. Address the ball with a slight bending at the knees and from the waist.
5. Make a full turn on the backswing with no body sway or lessening of grip pressure.

6. Swing the club back with a unified, one-piece motion. Avoid early cocking of the wrists.
7. Exercises will add distance.
8. Don't take too much advice from non-professionals.

—-from *Gary Player's Golf Secrets* by Gary Player

More Tips and Wisdom from Tommy Armour

1. It is not solely the capacity to make great shots that makes champions, but the essential quality of making very few bad shots.
2. Play the shot you've got the greatest chance of playing well, and play the shot that makes the next shot easy.
3. Every golfer scores better when he learns his capabilities.
4. Action before thought is the ruination of most of your shots.
5. The average player tees the ball too low for the drive. The fine player tees the ball high, usually with about half of the ball being above the top of the driver when it is soled behind the ball.
6. One thing I always advise is to use a club with a shaft a little bit whippier than you might want it to be. The big idea is to have the club working for you, instead of against you.
7. The majority of short putts are missed by looking for imaginary slopes and hitting the ball softly, trying to "baby" it into the cup.
8. Every good player steps up to a shot knowing exactly how he's going to hit the ball.
9. Think what to DO. That's concentration in golf.
10. The basic factor in all good golf is the grip. Get it right, and all other progress follows.
11. The Delphic "Know thyself" can be expanded for the golfer with other essential advice: " Know your clubs."

—-from *How to Play Your Best Golf All the Time* by Tommy Armour

Billy Casper: Shotmaking Strategy 101

1. Golf is a game of thought and management, with a premium on placement, accuracy, judgment and finesse.
2. Play safe and play within yourself.
3. Don't be too impatient or greedy. Consider the variables, the margins for error, then go with the percentage shots.
4. Play every shot so that the next one will be the easiest that you can give yourself.
5. Play easily, smoothly and unhurriedly.
6. Don't swing too hard or go for shots with little chance of success.

7. Know your limitations and play within them.

—from *The Methods of Golf's Masters*:
"Play Safe and Play Within Yourself" by Ken Bowden

Shotmaking Strategy/Advanced

1. If the pin is in the right hand side of the green, the shot goes from left to right.
2. If the pin is in the left, the shot goes from right to left.
3. If the pin is in the front of the green, the shot goes in high.
4. If the pin is in the back, the shot goes in lower. Never go in high to a pin in the back; always keep the ball under the hole. Never hit a full shot to a pin in the back; hit a soft, lower shot to get up to the pin.
5. Always drop down a club when in doubt. If you're between a 7 and an 8, take 7; between 6 and 7, take 6.
6. Never fight your eye when you look at a hole. If it looks one way, play it that way. Don't make a big deal out of an easy shot.
7. If a hole doesn't fit your eye, create a shot—-create something with a club you wouldn't ordinarily use.
8. On a medium length par 4, fit the shot to the fairway. Don't exert yourself. Put the shot in play with your regular swing in slow motion.
9. Always overclub downwind.
10. When trying to keep the shot down out of the wind, hit the ball on the second groove of the clubface.

—from *The Hogan Mystique* by Alexander, Anderson, Crenshaw and Venturi

Thoughts for Efficient Golf

"The general who wins a battle makes many cal-
culations in his temple before the battle is
fought." —Sun Tzu

1. Play from tees according to your ability.
2. Play at a pace within your comfort zone, but always tend toward fast rather than slow.
3. An effective shot is rarely the most glamorous shot.
4. There is a difference between confidence and cockiness.
5. We all take golf personally. The game will get to you from time to time, but you must leave the bad feeling behind as quickly as you can.
6. Keep things in perspective. Find a way to enjoy the hours you spend on the course.
7. Find a mentor.

8. Forget about winter rules. Golf is not designed to be played on a perfect surface.
9. Simple strategies breed success.
10. Be yourself.
11. Play the shot that is easiest for you.
12. Putting is more speed than line or stroke.
13. Never aim for a hazard.
14. Never try to force things.
15. Take a long-term approach to improvement.
16. Be patient.
17. Persevere.
18. Learn a swing that will keep the ball in play.
19. Don't ever think that you can understand the golf swing 100 percent.

—-from *The Swing* by Nick Price

Coping With Adversity

1. When in trouble, your first thought should be to escape. Don't try a miracle shot unless you need one to win.
2. Disregard bad shots and bad breaks. Other players are suffering the same fate.
3. Use a more lofted club from a bad lie because the ball will roll farther than normal.
4. In windy weather:
    —Keep shots to the green low, regardless of wind direction.
    —Don't fight a crosswind by hooking or slicing into it.
5. In wet weather:
    —Hang a towel from one of the ribs on the underside of your umbrella.
    —Use the towel to dry your hands and the club both before and after each shot.
    —Play all shots off the left heel to obtain maximum flight.
6. A slow, short backswing is helpful in maintaining balance and footing in both wind and rain.
7. In extreme heat:
    —Wear a hat as a safeguard against heat prostration.
    —Wear white clothes because white reflects the sun's rays.
8. In cold weather:
    —Keep the body and hands as warm as possible.
    —Flicking your fingers before each shot helps the blood circulate.
    —Balls with less compression are better than those which are tightly wound.

—-from *Gary Player's Golf Secrets* by Gary Player

Getting Up and Down

General Rules for Chips and Pitches

1. Club selection is crucial. The majority of golfers should use different clubs for different situations and lies. Simply let the club's normal loft do the work rather than use a different and sometimes more difficult swing technique.
2. Always spot-chip and spot-pitch, which means aiming at a point on the green where you want the ball to land and letting it run from there to the target.
3. Always try to land the ball on the green. This prevents bad bounces in the longer, uneven fringe and rough turf around the green.
4. Try not to land the ball on any severe slope—-uphill, downhill or side-hill. It is harder to judge the angle of the bounce from these slopes. Land the ball on flat areas of the green whenever possible.

Chipping Fundamentals

1. Set your hands ahead of the clubhead.
2. Grip down on your chipping clubs for control.
3. Just brush the grass.
4. Start the forward swing with the right knee moving toward the target. You'll get a good, positive acceleration of the clubhead.
5. Leave the flagstick in when chipping: it gives a backstop; it helps depth perception when sizing up the shot and figuring the distance; on longer chips, it eliminates any doubts about seeing the hole clearly.
6. Use a putter instead of chipping whenever possible.

Pitching Fundamentals

1. Weight favors the left foot and is centered on the balls of the feet.
2. Knees are slightly flexed and rear end stuck out so upper body and arms can hang over the ball.
3. Firm up your wrist action by "wearing splints." The great pitchers in the game use very little hand and wrist action.
4. Do not stand still and use just your hands and arms. Use your hips and knees in the swing. Lack of movement in the lower body ("cement legs") causes an inconsistent club path through impact.
5. Accelerate the clubhead, but don't overswing.
6. Make an underhanded motion.
7. Avoid backspin. Play pitches with as little spin as possible, because spin is hard to control and predict.

—-from *Getting Up and Down* by Tom Watson

Tips for Determining Grain Direction

1. Dull or Shiny? When the grain of the grass is running toward you, the putting surface will appear dull or dark. When the grain is running away from you, it appears lighter or shinier.
2. Away from Mountains. In a mountainous or hilly area, you can count on the grain running away from the mountains or down the slopes.
3. Toward Water. On seaside courses the grain will tend to run toward the water.
4. With the Wind. Where there are strong prevailing winds, the grain will tend to run in the direction in which the wind blows.
5. Toward the Setting Sun. Grass will tend to grow in the direction of the setting sun.
6. Lip is Indicator. By closely examining the edge or lip of a freshly cut cup, you will see that the side toward which the grain is growing is lined with cleanly clipped blades of grass. On the other side of the cup, you will see a line of dirt.

—-*Golf Digest* /October, 1975

Mind Over Putter/Putting Thoughts From John Updike

Putting: Is there an area of this fascinating game more apparently straight-forward, or one wherein the experienced golfer more ingeniously defeats himself?

1. Relax. It's only a game. Hold the putter lightly, so it can impart momentum and direction to the ball.
2. Having determined the line through visualization, hit the ball as if it's a straight putt. Don't stare or plumb-bob forever, but don't hurry either; wait that extra half-second until the projected putt becomes real in the mind.
3. Feel the clubhead moving close to the turf and the ball hugging the turf in its gravity-bound flight. This Earth-mysticism (*Erdschluss*) translates into a bold yet tactile stroke.
4. Challenge yourself with the notion that putts should be made. Perennial bogey shooters think of an automatic two-putt even from modest distances. This defeatist thinking breeds those dreadful three-putts.
5. Pretend that you've already been conceded the putt. Ever notice how easy it is to sink the putt on the second carefree attempt? Put the first try behind you in your mind, and rap the second one in.

—-from *Golf Digest*/February 1985: "Putting Thoughts" by John Updike

Putting Tenets/Moe Norman

He is arguably the greatest ball striker ever. Moe Norman's putting philosophy is equally unique and perceptive.

1. Trust what you see on the first glance.
2. If you think too much about a putt, you're prone to read too much into it.
3. If you're not sure about the break, just hit it at the hole.

—-from *The Feeling of Greatness* by Tim O'Connor

Visualization Procedure

"Don't try to keep your eye on the ball—-keep your mind on it—-and not on some bunker or pond on ahead." —-Jim Barnes

1. Line up your shot.
2. Decide on the proper flight that the ball must take to go where you want it to go.
3. As you prepare to hit the ball, IMAGINE the ball describing the flight pattern you have visualized, right to the hole
4. EXPECT the ball to follow your mental plan for it.

—-from *40 Common Errors…* by Arthur Shay

"Trouble exists, but you make sure in your thinking and visualization of the shot you want to hit that the shot is *to* some place. It's never *away* from anything. It has got to be positive. You play to something rather than away from something else…So much of this game is self-sabotage…Too often we talk ourselves out of it. We second guess. We play only half there…If you feel afraid, or hesitant, don't make the shot. Back off and see something else. You can't play golf with a frightened heart. Back off until your heart's totally there."
—-Debbie Massey

The Power of Positive Optimism

"I'm constantly thinking my way into mediocrity."

—-William Hallberg

1. Catch yourself doing something right and you will be amazed how you will start to do more things that are right. Once you get down on yourself in golf, you are through.
2. Golf is 50 percent bitter and the other 90 percent is sweet.
3. Anything worth doing does not have to be done perfectly at first.

4. It is not only important to think positively, but to believe and act positively. Many golfers head up to the ball to hit a shot with low energy. They look defeated before they start.
5. The worst a game of golf can be is great.
6. You are the sole judge of your goals. Don't dance to someone else's music.
7. When things aren't going right, patience is an energized belief that things will eventually go your way. As a result, you don't give up and start to cheat or lose control or begin to take unwarranted risks to get the results you want right now.
8. The best time orientation you can have over a golf shot is the precious present. Just hit it!

—-from *Playing the Great Game of Golf* by Ken Blanchard

Rotella Rules
1. People by and large become what they think about themselves.
2. A person with great dreams can achieve great things.
3. A player must accept the results of any shot, no matter how bad, and go on to the next one.
4. You cannot hit the ball consistently well if you think about the mechanics of your swing as you play.
5. Select the shot you know you can hit, not the shot Arnold Palmer (or John Daly) would hit. Have a conservative strategy and a cocky swing.

—-from *Golf Digest/*May 1995: "Think Like A Pro" by Bob Rotella

How to Play Bunker Shots
1. Establish a firm footing.
2. Take an open stance.
3. Open the clubface to match the address position.
4. Start with the weight favoring the left side.
5. Swing the club back like a "cut pitch shot."
6. Strike the sand from two to four inches behind the ball.
7. Do not let the clubface close through impact.
8. Accelerate through the ball to a natural finish.

—-from www.pga.com

Chiropractic Golf Tips
1. Stretch before playing: fingers, ankles, shoulders, hips, knees.
2. Warm up in both directions: right handed swings and left handed swings

alternatively.

3. Do not hit more than 25 balls on the range before playing. Better still: never hit more than 25 balls on the range.
4. Always bend from the knees when teeing up the ball, retrieving putts, replacing divots and picking up your bag.
5. Push your tee into the ground with your ball.
6. Arch your lower back 5 times before and after putting, especially on the practice green.
7. If you carry your clubs, use a Sunday bag; lighten your bag by leaving out unnecessary clubs.
8. If you use a handcart (trolley), push the cart.
9. Abstain from riding carts.
10. Replace metal spikes with soft spikes.
11. Use clubs with flexible shafts and soft grips.

How to Make a Hole in 9

1. Miss a short putt on the preceding green.
2. Advance to the next tee thinking about that missed short putt while applying every known epithet to the game of golf.
3. Brood over that missed putt, thinking about it exclusively as you lash at your tee shot with a tight grip and fast backswing.
4. Drive the first ball out of bounds.
5. Top your next drive into the rough. (You are now lying 3).
6. Slash away at your recovery shot in a manner comparable to your drives. (You should now also be thinking about the drive out of bounds and the topped drive as well as the missed putt).
7. You will now find your ball in a heel print in a fairway bunker. (You are lying 4).
8. Curse the heel print and hammer away at the sand. (You should reach the green in 6).
9. Rap your first putt with a reckless disregard for distance and direction. (You should be about 12 feet past the hole).
10. Lag your second putt to about 4 feet from the hole. (You are now lying 8).
11. Hit the ball carelessly with one hand as you pick it up and concede yourself the putt. (This will make 9).
11. Never make the mistake of calming down and concentrating on the next shot to be played because it may cut two or more strokes off your score for the hole.

—from *The Duffer's Handbook of Golf* by Grantland Rice and Clare Briggs

Speed Golf Tips

1. Wear running shoes instead of golf shoes.
2. Eschew practice swings.
3. Don't read putts.
4. Forget about posing after a sweetly struck shot.

> Note: Speed Golf is a hybrid of two sports: distance running and golf. You hit your ball, you run to it, you hit again. When you've completed 18 holes, you're done. Your score is computed by adding your elapsed time to the number of strokes taken, e.g. if you take 90 minutes to play and you shoot 80, your score is 170 in Speed Golf. Players adhere to all but two U.S.G.A. rules—-they do not remove the flagstick when putting and they are not required to re-play a lost ball from its original position. Speed Golf enthusiast Jay Larson says: "Sports are about rhythm. Slow golf steals that aspect of the game."
>
> —-from *Sky* / October 1998:
> "Speed Golf" by Michael Konik

Medieval Golf Instruction

> "Eschew the implement of correction and vitiate the golfling."
>
> —St. Francis of Niblicke

1. If ye are not able to hole putts, brew a potion consisting of hickory stump water, parsley, sage, rosemary and balata. Immerse thy putterhead in the potion for a fortnight. Remove thy putter from the magical elixir and consume the potion. Thy putting malady shalt be permanently exorcised.
2. If ye slice yere tee ball, ye should be confined to a dungeon. Solitary confinement for one month will eliminate slicing if ye are sound of character. If ye are lacking in moral turpitude, longer confinement is compulsory.
3. When attempting to extricate thy ball from watery filth, remove thy suit of armor and likewise remove whatsoever other physical encumbrances thee might possess.
4. If wizardry is not yere predilection, ye must avoid bunkers and other sandy entrapments.
5. Thou drivest for spectacle whilst thou puttest for farthings.
6. Spring forewarde, fall backe, chip in and putt out.
7. "I golfe, therefore I am." —Rene Decartes

8. Attempting to rescue a damsel from distress whilst sinking a putt shalt exact a three stroke penalty..
9. Besmirching the name of Sir Arnold of Palmer is punishable by pinioning on the rack.

Club-Throwing Technique 101

1. Aim. Always throw a club down the fairway, never behind you or straight up.
2. Alignment. The initial impulse to throw a club will come at the end of your follow-through. This is not a good position from which to launch a club. Instead, bring your right foot forward and square it with your left on a line perpendicular to the intended line of club flight so that your body is facing directly down the fairway.
3. Grip. Grip the club firmly but not tightly in your right hand (if you're right-handed); with the V formed by the thumb and forefinger pointing toward your right shoulder.
4. Forward Press. It is definite and pronounced.
5. Load and Fire Your Right Side. Your right arm goes straight back and your upper body rocks slightly toward the rear as your right side "loads up." Your right leg, bent slightly to maintain balance, now uncoils and your right arm whips forward.
6. Three-Quarters Overhand. Beginners and intermediates will find that a three-quarters overhand throw is easier to control.
7. Caution: No Sidewinders! A sidearm throw causes the club to rotate in the air parallel to the ground like a scythe, endangering everything in its path. Moreover, the slightest miscalculation of the proper release point could cause the club to shoot out sideways rather than forward and maim a member of your foursome.
8. Plant and Release. The club should be released as the left foot is planted and at a point when the extended right arm is at approximately two o'clock. A club must be released much higher than a baseball, lest the twirling clubhead strike the ground too forcefully and snap off at the hosel. The idea is to throw the club, not destroy it.
9. Keep Your Eye on the Club. Nothing is more embarrassing than throwing a club and then having to ask a playing partner where it went.
—-from *Divots, Shanks, Gimmes, Mulligans, and Chili Dips* by Glen Waggoner

Advanced Club-Throwing Techniques: Opponent's Club
When your opponent hits a terrible shot and starts cursing a blue streak…

1. Heartily empathize with his anger at the flub.

2. Get really worked up and insist that a player of his caliber can hardly be expected to play decently with inferior equipment.
3. Grab his club and throw it in the woods.
4. Shout "good riddance" as it windmills into the beyond.
5. Assure your opponent in a friendly way that he is better off without the club.

(Note: This is an especially useful strategy in match-play if the club in question is a putter and you toss it into a water hazard early in the round).

—from *Bad Golf My Way* by Nielsen and Beard

The Five Basic Swing Types: Which One are You?

In the September 1990 issue of **Golf**, Mike Adams and Bill Moretti isolate basic swing types. It is their contention that every golfer fits one of these descriptions.

1. Reroute and Hold.
2. Rock and Slide.
3. Turn and Connect.
4. Slide and Slap.
5. Tilt and Block.

The astute analysis by Adams and Moretti overlooks the following common swing techniques.

1. Dip, Rip, Nip and Skip.
2. Lift and Separate.
3. Reverse Pivot and Fat Divot.
4. Pronate and Exacerbate.
5. Moving and Peeking.

I solemnly swear on my honor that I will thoroughly and painstakingly demonstrate each of these movements when I appear with Oprah (weather permitting).

Happy Golfing!

IV. Handy Reference Lists

Here they are. A multiplicitous conglomeration of lies, damn lies and statistics...the mundane and the trivial...all under one roof for your delectation and perusal. Go ahead. Be a glutton. Feast on lists that are guaranteed to be fat free and contain no calories. Furthermore, all lists are individually formatted to meet USGA guidelines for initial velocity and launch angle.

Let the frivolity begin...

LPGA Founding Members

The LPGA was chartered in September 1950. There were twelve founding members.

1. Alice Bauer
2. Marlene Bauer
3. Patty Berg, president
4. Helen Dettweiler
5. Opal Hill
6. Betty Jameson
7. Sally Sessions
8. Marilyn Smith
9. Shirley Spork
10. Louise Suggs
11. Betty Mims White
12. Babe Zaharias

The *Power-Bilt* Professional Panel/1967

1. Miller Barber
2. Frank Beard
3. Gene Bone

4. Frank Boynton
5. Gay Brewer
6. Ed Davis
7. Gloria Ehret
8. Jim Ferriell
9. Bill Kaiser
10. Sandra McClinton
11. Bobby Nichols
12. Ed Whalley

—-from 1967 *POWER-BILT* Catalogue

How to Spot a Hustler

1. Get a look at your opponent's left hand. If there's a visible callus across the base of the ring finger and the little finger, think again.
2. Beware of anyone whose suntan is darker than your tan.
3. Be wary of opponents who distract you with multiple side wagers and confusing gimmick bets.
4. Give a wide berth to anyone who's always telling you how good your playing.
5. Never wager with a sick opponent. A player who's hurting doesn't have room in his mind for anything but his golf game.
6. You can't win against an unemployed golfer. Either he doesn't have any money or he practices all day.
7. Never play a golfer with a 1-iron in his bag.
8. Run away from a golfer who asks for fewer strokes than he's been getting and at the same time wants to increase the bet.

—-from *Pigeons, Marks, Hustlers and Other Golf Bettors You Can Beat*
by Sam Snead and Jerry Tarde

The Legends of Golf

1. 1978 Sam Snead/Gardner Dickinson   193
2. 1979 Julius Boros/Roberto De Vicenzo   195
3. 1980 Tommy Bolt/Art Wall   187
4. 1981 Gene Littler/Bob Rosburg   257
5. 1982 Sam Snead/Don January   183
6. 1983 Rod Funseth/Roberto De Vicenzo   258
7. 1984 Billy Casper/Gay Brewer   258
8. 1985 Don January/Gene Littler   257
9. 1986 Don January/Gene Littler   255
10. 1987 Bruce Crampton/Orville Moody   251

11. 1988 Bruce Crampton/Orville Moody	254
12. 1989 Harold Henning/Al Geiberger	251
13. 1990 Dale Douglass/Charles Coody	249
14. 1991 Lee Trevino/Mike Hill	252
15. 1992 Lee Trevino/Mike Hill	251
16. 1993 Harold Henning*	204
17. 1994 Dale Douglass/Charles Coody	188
18. 1995 Lee Trevino/Mike Hill	195
19. 1996 Lee Trevino/Mike Hill	198
20. 1997 John Bland/Graham Marsh	192
21. 1998 Dale Douglass/Charles Coody	192
22. 1999 Gil Morgan/Hubert Green	194
23. 2000 Jim Colbert/Andy North	191
24. 2001 Jim Colbert/Andy North	124
25. 2002 Bruce Lietzke/Bill Rogers	124
26. 2003 Gary Koch/Roger Maltbie	130

*Harold Henning held the unique distinction as the only individual champion of the Legends of Golf (1993). He also won the event with partner Al Geiberger in 1989. The sponsorship quickly realized their error following the 1993 tournament and reinstated the highly entertaining team format. In the esteemed opinion of Donald "Skippy" Miller, Esq., the Legends of Golf is indisputably the most entertaining Senior tournament on the schedule. It is a tragedy of profound proportions that the tournament was once again altered to medal play in 2002 although a modified team format (the Raphael Division) remains in force. Let's hear it for the team: T-E-A-M, RAH Team!!

Shell's Wonderful World of Golf/ Marquee Performers, 1962-'70

Shell's Wonderful World of Golf premiered in 1962 and continued for 9 glorious years in its initial incarnation. Roberto De Vicenzo, winner of more than 200 international tournaments including the 1967 British Open at Royal Liverpool (a.k.a. Hoylake), competed in more Shell matches than any other player. Here is the breakdown of the most prolific Shell performers with their total number of exhibitions and the year they first appeared on *Shell's Wonderful World of Golf*.

1. Roberto De Vicenzo, 11 (1962)
2. Sanders, 7 (1963)
3. Billy Casper, 6 (1962)
4. George Knudson, 6 (1964)

5. Frank Beard, 6 (1969)
6. Sam Snead, 5 (1963)
7. Julius Boros, 5 (1964)
8. Dan Sikes, 5 (1969)
9. Gene Littler, 4 (1962)
10. Peter Allis, 4 (1963)
11. Tony Lema, 4 (1964)
12. Dave Marr, 4 (1964)
13. Chi Chi Rodriguez, 4 (1964)
14. Ben Arda, 4 (1966)

Rules of 1754

I. You must tee your ball within a club length of the hole.

II. Your tee must be upon the ground.

III. You are not to change the ball that you strike off the tee.

IV. You are not to remove stones, bones, or any break club for sake of playing your ball, except upon the fair green, and that only within a clublength of your ball.

V. If your ball comes among water, or any watery filth, you are at liberty to take out your ball, and throw it behind the hazard, six yards at least; you may play it with any club, and allow your adversary a stroke for so getting out your ball.

VI. If your balls be found anywhere touching one another, you are to lift the first ball till you play the last.

VII. At holing, you are to play your ball honestly for the hole, and not to play upon your adversary's ball, not lying in your way to the hole.

VIII. If you should lose your ball by its being taken up, or in any other way, you are to go back to the spot where you struck last, and drop another ball, and allow your adversary a stroke for the misfortune.

IX. No man, at holing his ball, is to be allowed to mark to the hole with his club or anything else.

X. If a ball be stopped by any person, horse, dog, or anything else, the ball so stopped must be played where it lies.

XI. If you draw your club in order to strike, and proceed so far in the stroke as to be bringing down your club—if then your club shall break in any way it is to be accounted a stroke.

XII. He whose ball lies farthest from the hole is obliged to play first.

XIII. Neither trench, ditch, nor dike made for the preservation of the links, nor the scholars' holes, nor the soldiers' lines, shall be accounted a hazard, but the ball is to be taken out, teed and played with any iron club.
    —The Honourable Company of Edinburgh Golfers

K.I.S.S. Rules

Play the course as you find it.
Play the ball as it lies.
If neither is possible,
do whatever is fair and equitable.

Integrity

The integrity and sportsmanship of its competitors characterize the great game of golf. Among the extraordinary champions of the game, one player above all other exemplifies this ideal.

Bob Jones

Jones called penalties on himself for minor violations of the Rules in four national championships. In the 1925 U.S. Open, he penalized himself when his ball accidentally moved slightly in the rough. No one else saw the ball move, but Jones insisted on imposing the penalty. That stroke cost him the title and conceivably prevented him from becoming the only competitor ever to win five U.S. Open Championships. Jones became indignant when praised for his adherence to the Rules. "You might as well praise a man for not robbing a bank," he said.

G. Peper's 10 Detestable Rules

1. Rule 4-4: Maximum of 14 clubs. That's way too many.
2. Rule 5-3: Ball unfit for play. Play it until the next tee.
3. Rule 10: Order of play. Play ready golf——if you're ready, hit the damn ball.
4. Rule 13-4C: Ball in hazard. The Brits have a Local Rule that allows removal of interfering stones. For the sake of safety, as well as sanity, we need a similar rule.
5. Rule 14-3: Artificial devices. Why prohibit the use of electronic yardage calculators? They're fast and accurate.
6. Rule 16-18: Lifting a ball on the putting green. What is more imbecilic than a player who lifts, cleans and meticulously positions his ball, then strokes a 20-footer to within a foot of the hole, and before tapping in, he lifts, cleans and positions his ball again? To that end, a ball on the putting green should be lifted and cleaned *once*.
7. Rule 16-1F: Position of caddie. Get the read from your caddie and get

him out of there before you address the ball. And let's apply this rule to all shots, not just putts.

8. Rule 17-3C: Ball striking flagstick. If I'm on the edge of the green and you're on the fringe, why should you have the option of leaving the flag in while I don't? As recently as the 1950s, there was no penalty for striking the flag stick from any distance. Let's go back to that. We'll save strokes and time.

9. Rule 22: Ball interfering with or assisting play. Currently you may lift and mark your ball if you think the unmarked ball might help your opponent. Let's return to the practice where players are allowed to make use of their opponent's ball as a backstop or target. This would enhance strategy and intrigue around the green.

10. Rule 1-4: Amateur status. Enough said.

—from "10 Rules I Hate" by G. Peper, *Golf Magazine*/October 1998

Proper Golf Etiquette

"Its code of conduct makes golf the greatest game of all."

—Arnold Palmer

1. Don't talk, stand close or move around when another player is hitting.
2. Don't hit a shot when another player is within range.
3. Don't mark a scorecard on the green.
4. Don't waste time pacing off yardages.
5. Don't lean on your putter when waiting to putt.
6. Always be ready to play when it's your turn.
7. Always lay the flagstick down off the green when putting.
8. Always lay your bag down off the green when putting.
9. Always replace the flagstick in the hole before leaving the green.
10. Always replace your divots.
11. Always rake the sand in a bunker after hitting from the bunker.
12. Always repair ballmarks on the putting green.
13. Always leave the course in good condition.
14. Always wave the group behind through if your own group is playing slowly and there is an open hole ahead. (Never ask to play through or bully your way through a slow moving group. Such obnoxious, rude and contentious behavior is contrary to the spirit of the game. Only play through when you receive an invitation to do so).
15. Show absolute sportsmanship and honesty. It is the heart and soul of the game.

—from *Golf Magazine/December 1998: "Behave Yourself"*

The Azalea Open Invitational

1949 -
1950 –E. J. Harrison
1951 –Lloyd Mangrum
1952 –Jimmy Clark
1953 –Jerry Barber
1954 –Bob Toski
1955 –Billy Maxwell
1956 –Mike Souchak
1957 –Arnold Palmer
1958 –Howie Johnson
1959 –Art Wall, Jr.
1960 –Tom Nieporte
1961 –Jerry Barber
1962 –Dave Marr
1963 –Jerry Barber
1964 –Al Besselink
1965 –Dick Hart
1966 –Bert Yancey
1967 -
1968 -
1969 –Dale Douglass
1970 –Cesar Sanudo

Designed by Donald Ross in 1928, the par 71, 6,567 yard Cape Fear Country Club in Wilmington, North Carolina was the elegant setting for the Azalea Open from 1949 to 1970.

Please fill in the blank spaces with the names of the tournament winners for 1949, 1967 and 1968. I apologize to the unidentified victors and I vow to amend this oversight in *Hole-In-One Pair of Pants* (Volume ii).

Virtues of Golf (#10—27)

1. Golf is just a game. Games don't do anything to solve the world's problems, but they don't do very much to make them worse, either.
2. Golf is founded on honesty. It is the only professional sport in which players are expected to call penalties on themselves.
3. Playing eighteen holes with someone is a good way to take his or her measure. The game has a way of magnifying character flaws—-whininess, explosiveness, dishonesty, lack of charity, self-delusion—-which may be less readily detectable in nongolfing situations.

4. Golf is a social game. There is so much downtime during a typical round that partners can actually carry on real conversations between shots.
5. Golf is unusual among competitive sports in that it can be played alone.
6. Golf promotes a healthy sense of play. It is ideally suited to pretending.
7. Because of golf's handicapping system, players of greatly different levels of skill can play competitive matches.
8. Golf is a literate game. The **list** of distinguished chroniclers is impressively long.
9. Golf provides an organizing principle for travel.
10. Although expensive in absolute terms, on an hourly basis bowling is costlier than golf.
11. If you walk and play fairly quickly, golf provides a certain amount of exercise. Golf is a walk improved. Golf is a walk with a purpose.
12. Golf confers no particular advantage to extreme youth. Golf rewards experience, poise, and strategic resourcefulness, just as life does.
13. Golf is continually challenging. No matter how good your game may seem at some particular moment, there's always some part in need of tinkering. Furthermore, you always know that the parts that now seem sound may suddenly disintegrate.
14. Golf is a game of good and bad luck. It is played under circumstances that ensure superior skill alone will not always determine the victor.
15. Golf satisfies many the same testosterone-based male yearnings that hunting does, but without the bloodshed.
16. Golf can provide an agreeable alternative to marriage. The members of any club tend to pair off over time. The same guys play together week after week.
17. Golf keeps you interested in being alive.
18. Golf reminds you of your mortality. Like life, a round of golf begins in easy optimism, progresses through a lengthy middle period in which hope and despair are mingled, deteriorates into regret, confusion, and resignation, and comes abruptly to an end.

—from *My Usual Game* by David Owen

Dave Barry on Golf

"No book about golf in the modern era would be complete without some insights from Dave Barry." —unknown (Tom Sacks)

1. Golfers want to hit the ball the least possible number of times so they can return to the clubhouse to tell boring anecdotes and drink beer.
2. Golfers ride in electric carts to avoid the dangers of physical activity.

3. Golfers wear the most unattractive pants that money can buy, pants so ugly that they have to be manufactured by blind people in dark rooms.

4. After a swing the ball completely disappears. You look for it, but you never see it again. The ball has gone into another dimension, a parallel universe.

5. A golfer should complete nine holes in less time than it would take to memorize *Moby Dick* in Korean.

6. Fishing is similar to golf. In both sports you hold a long skinny thing in your hands while nothing happens for days at a time.

—-from *Dave Barry Turns 40* by Dave Barry

Multiple Women's Open Champions

1. Babe Zaharias; 1948, '50, '54
2. Louise Suggs; 1949, '52
3. Betsy Rawls; 1951, '53, '57, '60
4. Mickey Wright; **1958, '59**, '61, '64
5. Susie Berning; 1968, **'72, '73**
6. Donna Caponi; **1969, '70**
7. Joanne Carner; 1971, '76
8. Hollis Stacy; **1977, '78**, '84
9. Betsy King; **1989, '90**
10. Patty Sheehan; 1992, '94
11. Annika Sorenstam; **1996, '97**
12. Karrie Webb; **2000, '01**
13. Juli Inkster; 1999, '02

For the uninformed: x, x+1 equals **bold**, i.e. repeat champions.

In addition to winning the Open Championship twice, both Louise Suggs and Joanne Carner have been five time runners up. I'm certain that both of these great champions would agree with my contention that anyone who has triumphed in two or more U.S. Open Championships should automatically gain entry into the Hall of Fame.

Multiple U.S. Open Champions

> "Any player can win a U.S. Open, but it takes a helluva player to win two."
>
> —Walter Hagen

1. Willie Anderson; 1901, **'03, '04, 05**
2. Alex Smith; 1906, '10

3. John McDermott; **1911, '12**
4. Walter Hagen; 1914, '19
5. Gene Sarazen; 1922, '32
6. Bobby Jones; 1923, '26, **'29, '30**
7. Ralph Guldahl; **1937, '38**
8. Ben Hogan; 1948, **'50, '51**, '53
9. Cary Middlecoff; 1949, '56
10. Julius Boros; 1952, '63
11. Billy Casper; 1959, '66
12. Jack Nicklaus; 1962, '67, '72, '80
13. Lee Trevino; 1968, '71
14. Hale Irwin; 1974, '79, '90
15. Andy North; 1978, '85
16. Curtis Strange; **1988, '89**
17. Ernie Els; 1994, '97
18. Lee Janzen; 1993, '98
19. Payne Stewart; 1991, '99
20. Tiger Woods; 2000, '02

Willie Anderson accomplished the only three-peat in Open history, 1903—'05.

Men's U.S. Amateur Medal Play CHAMPIONS (1965—1972)

1965 — Bob Murphy
1966 — Gary Cowan
1967 — Bob Dickson
1968 — Bruce Fleisher
1969 — Steve Melnyk
1970 — Lanny Wadkins
1971 — Gary Cowan
1972 — Vinny Giles

Multiple U.S. Amateur Champions

"Only a truly extraordinary competitor can accomplish the remarkable feat of winning two (or more) U.S. Amateurs."

—Donald Miller

1. H. J. Whigham; 1896; '97
2. Walter J. Travis; 1900, '01, '03

3. H. Chandler Egan; 1904, '05
4. Jerome D. Travers; 1907, '08, '12, '13
5. Francis Ouimet, 1914, '31
6. Robert A. Gardner; 1909, '15
7. Charles Evans, Jr.; 1916, '20
8. Robert T. Jones, Jr.; 1924, '25, '27, '28, '30
9. W. Lawson Little; 1934, '35
10. William P. Turnesa; 1938, '48
11. Marvin H. Ward; 1939, '41
12. Charles R. Coe; 1949, '58
13. E. Harvie Ward; 1955, '56
14. Jack Nicklaus; 1959, '61
15. Deane Beman; 1960, '63
16. Gary Cowan; 1966, '71
17. Jay Sigel; 1982, '83
18. Tiger Woods; 1994, '95, '96

The oldest championship in the U.S., the Amateur has been a match play competition except for an eight-year period from 1965—1972 when it was conducted at stroke play. Gary Cowan is the only competitor among the multiple champions who did not triumph in match play.

The Greatest Opens Ever
1. Philadelphia CC, 1939
2. Oakland Hills CC, 1951
3. Cherry Hills CC, 1960
4. Interlachen CC, 1930
5. The Country Club, 1913
6. Riviera CC, 1948
7. Oakmont CC, 1962
8. Scioto CC, 1926
9. Canterbury GC, 1940
10. Baltusrol GC, 1980

—Dan Jenkins, *Golf Digest*/June 1995

Senior Tour/Debut Winners
This is the short—but impressive—list of players who were victorious in their inaugural Senior Tour event.

1. Don January (1980)

2. Roberto De Vicenzo (1980)
3. Arnold Palmer (1980)
4. Rod Funseth (1983)
5. Gary Player (1985)
6. George Archer (1989)
7. Jack Nicklaus (1990)
8. Tom Weiskopf (1993)
9. Bruce Fleisher (1999)
10. Lanny Wadkins (2000)
11. Andy North (2000)
12. Bobby Wadkins (2001)

In February 1999, Mr. Fleisher became the first Senior Tour player to achieve victories in his first two appearances among the "50 and over" fraternity.

Basic Rules of Landscape Architecture
1. Plant trees in groups of three or more; odd numbers are more pleasing to the eye.
2. Plant trees of different species to ensure disease problems do not wipe out an entire planting. Stick to species native to the area.
3. Avoid formal arrangement of plants. It looks out of place in the naturalized landscape of golf, and a single loss destroys the form.
4. Use primarily deciduous trees unless evergreens dominate the site. Shrubs or evergreens that branch low to the ground block recovery shots and should be reserved for use as safety screens or visual buffers at the boundary of the course.
5. Plant a few large specimen trees instead of several smaller ones. Committees often make the mistake of planting small trees too close together and have to thin them out in a few years.
6. Avoid plantings that will excessively shade greens and tees.
7. Avoid trees with shallow roots or litter problems.
8. Avoid planting trees at the inside corner of a dogleg hole, or near the landing area of the fairway. Such placement leaves the question of whether the second shot is blocked by the trees a matter of luck. Trees located between landing areas, on the contrary, will affect the trajectory of the second shot in proportion to the error of the drive.
9. Avoid planting trees in the same pattern on each hole. Trees should add visual variety to individual holes.
10. Do not plant shrubs as yardage markers at the edge of the fairway. They look unnatural and they are a nuisance when mowing the rough.

—from *The Anatomy of a Golf Course* by Tom Doak

First Ten Golfers to Earn $1,000,000 (in order of occurrence)

1. Arnold Palmer
2. Billy Casper
3. Jack Nicklaus
4. Lee Trevino
5. Bruce Crampton
6. Gary Player
7. Tom Weiskopf
8. Gene Littler
9. Johnny Miller
10. Miller Barber

All-Time PGA Tour Money Leaders (01-01-90)

1. Tom Kite $5,600,691
2. Tom Watson $5,160,243
3. Jack Nicklaus $5,102,420
4. Curtis Strange $5,015,720
5. Ben Crenshaw $4,115,074
6. Lanny Wadkins $3,940,949
7. Ray Floyd $3,616,587
8. Payne Stewart $3,606,707
9. Lee Trevino $3,460,416
10. Hale Irwin $3,227,831

All-Time PGA Tour Money Leaders (01-01-00)

1. Greg Norman $12,507,322
2. Davis Love III $12,487,463
3. Payne Stewart $11,737,008
4. Nick Price $11,386,236
5. Tiger Woods $11,315,128
6. Fred Couples $11,305,069
7. Mark O'Meara $11,182,269
8. Tom Kite $10,533,102
9. Scott Hoch $10,308,995
10. David Duval $10,047,947

All-Time PGA Tour Money Leaders (01-01-01)

1. Tiger Woods $20,503,450
2. Davis Love III $14,825,227

3.	Phil Mickelson	$13,434,115
4.	Nick Price	$13,190,669
5.	Greg Norman	$13,087,832
6.	David Duval	$12,510,792
7.	Fred Couples	$12,295,284
8.	Hal Sutton	$12,162,000
9.	Payne Stewart	$11,737,008
10.	Scott Hoch	$11,677,883

L.A. Open / Multiple Winners

1. Harry Cooper; 1926, '37
2. Macdonald Smith; 1928, '29, '32, '34
3. Ben Hogan; 1942, '47, '48
4. Sam Snead; 1945, '50
5. Lloyd Mangrum; 1949, '51, '53, '56
6. Arnold Palmer; 1963, '66, '67
7. Paul Harney; 1964, '65
8. Billy Casper; 1968, '70
9. Gil Morgan; 1978, '83
10. Lanny Wadkins; 1979, '85
11. Tom Watson; 1980, '82
12. Fred Couples; 1990, '92
13. Corey Pavin; 1994, '95

The Top Eight Reasons Not to Practice Putting

1. Ben Hogan didn't.
2. It's no fun.
3. You either have the touch or you don't.
4. My long irons need work.
5. The practice green is too different from the greens on the course.
6. It doesn't seem to matter.
7. It hurts my back.
8. I don't have time.

—from *On Golf* by Jim Flick

The Essential Features of an Ideal Golf Course

1. The course should be arranged in two loops of nine holes.
2. There should be a large proportion of good two-shot holes, two or three drive-and-pitch holes, and at least four one-shot holes.

3. There should be little walking between the greens and tees.
4. Greens and fairways should be sufficiently undulating, but there should be no hill climbing.
5. Every hole should have a different character.
6. Blind approach shots should be kept to a minimum.
7. The course should have beautiful surroundings. All artificial features should have a natural appearance so that a stranger cannot distinguish them from nature itself.
8. There should be a sufficient number of heroic carries from the tee, but the course should be arranged so that the weaker player with the loss of a stroke or portion of a stroke shall always have an alternative route open to him.
9. There should be infinite variety in the strokes required to play the various holes.
10. There should be a complete absence of the annoyance and irritation caused by the necessity of searching for lost balls.
11. The course should be so interesting that even the most skillful player is constantly stimulated to improve his game in attempting shots that he has hitherto been unable to play.
12. The course should be arranged so that the high handicapper, or even the beginner, should be able to enjoy his round in spite of piling up a big score.
13. The course should be equally good during winter and summer. The fairways and greens should be well-manicured, and the approach areas should have the same consistency as the greens.

—from *Golf Architecture* by Dr. Alister MacKenzie

GOLF All-America

1964
Driver - Jack Nicklaus
Fairway Woods - Gary Player
Long Irons - Arnold Palmer
Middle Irons - Bobby Nichols
Short Irons - Ken Venturi
Pitching Wedge - Tony Lema
Sand Wedge - Julius Boros
Putter - Billy Casper

1965
Driver - Jack Nicklaus
Fairway Woods - Gary Player

Long Irons - Arnold Palmer
Middle Irons - Gene Littler
Short Irons - Tony Lema
Pitching Wedge - Dave Marr
Sand Wedge - Sam Snead
Putter - Billy Casper

1966
Driver - Jack Nicklaus
Fairway Woods - Al Geiberger
Long Irons - Arnold Palmer
Middle Irons - Doug Sanders
Short Irons - Gene Littler
Pitching Wedge - Gay Brewer
Sand Wedge - Julius Boros
Putter - Billy Casper

—from *Golf Magazine*/January 1967

40 Common Errors

1. Choosing the wrong club
2. Not warming up
3. Poor grip
4. Piccolo grip
5. Losing your grip
6. Flipping of hands
7. Stiff address
8. Poor set-up
9. Lifting the heel
10. Poor weight shift
11. Moving head
12. Head bobbing
13. Dipping
14. Poor aiming
15. Laying the club off
16. Flat-footed stance
17. Stance too wide
18. Takeaway troubles
19. Overswing
20. Incomplete backswing
21. Improper shoulder turn
22. Getting ahead of the ball

23. Swatting
24. Slicing
25. Hooking
26. Shanking
27. Scooping on pitch shots
28. Losing your chips
29. Making the rough rougher than it is
30. Sloping
31. Getting trapped
32. Wind troubles
33. Striking high obstacle
34. Playing a sunken ball
35. Obstacle to obstacle shot
36. Not reading the putting green
37. Poor eye position for putting
38. Hit or miss putting practice
39. Not visualizing your shot
40. Not concentrating

—*40 Common Errors in Golf and How to Correct Them*/Arthur Shay

Hagar the Horrible's Guide to S - L - O - W Play

…several ways to hinder a round of golf

1. Golf balls are expensive. Never stop looking for a lost ball till dark. Don't hit a provisional, as that just admits defeat.

2. Rules are important. All questions about them should be thoroughly thrashed out by the foursome whenever they arise.

3. Keep meticulous scores. Stay by the hole and carefully record all numbers. Settle all bets before going to the next tee. Don't let yourself be rushed at this important time.

4. Approach every putt with a fresh eye. Don't even start plumb-bobbing until it's your turn to putt. Then you can have the green entirely to yourself.

5. Don't let any groups play through your foursome, even if they are faster and there is a hole open in front of you. It muddles up the fairway.

6. Golf is a game of inches. Double-check the yardage markers to know exactly where you are and carefully mark off the distance between the marker and your ball.

7. You have a lot on your mind. Never miss an opportunity to check in with your office and call home to see how the children are.

8. If you have to walk across the fairway to get to your ball, don't tire yourself by taking more than one club with you.

9. Always play from the back tees.
10. Take a mulligan. In fact take several. Never leave the first tee until you're happy with your drive.
11. Always have lunch at the turn. Make sure to order a cheeseburger—well done.
12. We all need help on the course so never pass up a chance to give a lesson to your partner.

With time, lots of time, you can learn to play golf so slowly that NOBODY gets to enjoy the game.

—from *Golf Digest* / March 1988

The Wisdom of Donald Ross

1. It is absolutely futile to lay out a course on paper.
2. Man cannot do in a few days what nature took years to accomplish.
3. Make each hole present a different problem. Arrange it so that every stroke must be played with the full concentration and attention necessary to good golf.
4. There should be two ways to play a hole, one for the strong player, and one for the man who is not so strong.
5. The cardinal rule: make the holes so that the man who plays as he should gets par, and the man who makes a mistake get one more than par.
6. It is best if the first two holes or so are not too difficult. Give the player a chance to warm up and get his stroke under control. Then give him some real nuts to crack.
7. Provide at least one or two drive-and-pitch holes. These holes are delightful if properly constructed.
8. It has always seemed better to me to have a few very fine holes and the rest fair, than eighteen fair holes with none that leave a distinct impression on the player's mind.
9. A choice nine-hole course is better than an indifferent eighteen-hole course.
10. Give me some slightly rolling terrain and sandy soil, and I'll give you the best courses.
11. Select locations for putting greens to give desirable undulating surfaces. Nature does this sort of thing best.
12. There is no such thing as a misplaced bunker. Regardless of where a bunker might be, it is the business of the player to avoid it.
13. Water hazards lend variety to a course and test a player's skill, but don't allow enthusiasm for them to run away with good judgment. Limit the number of water hazards to three. Two might be better.

14. Blind shots are bound to occur on undulating land. One or two of them add a bit of spice to the game.

—-from *Golf Has Never Failed Me* by Donald Ross

Wall of Fame/A Profile of Art Wall, Jr.

Art Wall, Jr. was "an authoritative striker of the irons, and discerning spectators were equally impressed by his politeness and inveterate sincerity."

—Herbert Warren Wind

1. Birdied five of the last six holes (13,14,15,17,18) at Augusta National to win the 1959 Masters.
2. Career holes-in-one: 45.
3. Leading money winner, 1959: $53,167.
4. Player of the Year, 1959.
5. Vardon Trophy (1959):
6. The "unofficial" birth of the Senior Tour occurred on April 30, 1979 when Roberto De Vicenzo and Julius Boros defeated Tommy Bolt and ART WALL, Jr. in a sensational six hole sudden death play-off to earn a victory in the second edition of the Legends of Golf.
7. In 1980, Tommy Bolt and ART WALL shot a record 23 under par score of 187 to win the Legends of Golf tournament.
8. Wall lost the 1960 Western Open in a playoff with Canadian Stan Leonard.
9. Ryder Cup team: 1957, '59, '61.
10. In 1975, Art Wall won the Greater Milwaukee Open at age 51 to become the second oldest winner in PGA Tour history.
11. Art Wall won 8 tournaments on the (Seagrams) Caribbean Tour:

Caracas Open	1963, 1966
Maracaibo Open	1964, 1965, 1966
Los Lagartos International	1964
Panama Open	1965
Puerto Rico Open	1965

The Rankin File

...the exceptional career of Hall-of-Famer Judy Rankin

1. National PeeWee Champion, 1953—'56
2. Missouri Amateur Champion, 1959
3. Low amateur in Women's U.S. Open, 1960

4. Joined LPGA Tour at age 17, 1962
5. First victory: Corpus Christi Open, 1968
6. Won Colgate Dinah Shore Winner's Circle, 1976
7. Won six tournaments and set single-season earnings record of $150,734 (first LPGA player to exceed $100,000 threshold), 1976
8. Won Peter Jackson Classic, 1977
9. Leading money winner: $122,890, 1977
10. LPGA Player of the Year, 1976 and 1977
11. Vare Trophy: 1973 (73.08); 1976 (72.25); 1977 (72.16)
12. Set record for most top-10 finishes in one season with 25, 1977
13. European Open champion, 1974 and 1977
14. Joined ABC Sports as on-course commentator, 1984
15. Enshrined in LPGA Hall of Fame, 2000

—from *A Woman's Guide to Better Golf* by Judy Rankin

LPGA Majors
1. Western Open (1930—1967)
2. Titleholders Championship (1937—1972)
3. U.S. Open (1946—present)
4. LPGA Championship (1955—present)
5. du Maurier Classic (1979—2000)
6. Dinah Shore (1983—present)
7. British Open (2001—present)

Note: The Dinah Shore was first played in 1972, but it was not recognized as a Major until 1983; the du Maurier was first played in 1973 and became a Major in 1979. From 1973 through 1978, LPGA players competed in only two Majors annually. Judy Rankin, the dominant player of her era, played in only two majors per year during her competitive prime.

LPGA Majors: Victory Totals

1.	Patty Berg	15	(1-U.S. Open; 7-Titleholders; 7-Western Open)
2.	Mickey Wright	13	(4- U.S. Open; 4-LPGA; 2-Titleholders; 3-Western Open)
3.	Louise Suggs	11	(2-U.S. Open; 1-LPGA; 4-Titleholders; 4-Western Open)

| 4. | Babe Zaharias | 10 | (3-U.S. Open; 3-Titleholders; 4-Western Open) |
| 5. | Betsy Rawls | 8 | (4-U.S. Open; 2-LPGA; 2-Western Open) |

Dinah Shore Champions '72—'82

1. 1972 - Jane Blalock   213
2. 1973 - Mickey Wright   284
3. 1974 - Jo Ann Prentice   289
4. 1975 - Sandra Palmer   283
5. 1976 - Judy Rankin   285
6. 1977 - Kathy Whitworth   289
7. 1978 - Sandra Post   283
8. 1979 - Sandra Post   276
9. 1980 - Donna Caponi   275
10. 1981 - Nancy Lopez   277
11. 1982 - Sally Little   278

du Maurier Champions '73—'78

1. 1973 – Jocelyne Bourassa   214
2. 1974 – Carole Jo Callison   208
3. 1975 – JoAnne Carner   214
4. 1976 – Donna Caponi   212
5. 1977 – Judy Rankin   214
6. 1978 – JoAnne Carner   278

Discontinuance of Play

The player shall not discontinue play unless:

1. the Committee has suspended play
2. he believes there is danger from lightning
3. he is seeking a decision from the Committee on a doubtful or disputed point
4. there is some other good reason such as sudden illness

—Rule 6-8a, *The Official Rules of Golf*

Lightning Safety Tips

Avoid:
1. open areas
2. water
3. metal
4. wire fences, overhead wires and power lines
5. isolated trees
6. elevated ground
7. maintenance machinery
8. golf carts

Seek:
1. lightning shelters
2. clubhouse
3. maintenance buildings
4. large permanent buildings
5. automobiles

When one of the above is not available, seek:
6. dense woods
7. lowest elevation areas

   —from the United States Golf Association, Far Hills, N.J.

PGA Championship/Match Play Winners (1916-'57)

1916 - Jim Barnes
1917 - No Championship
1918 - No Championship
1919 - Jim Barnes (2)*
1920 - Jock Hutchinson (1)
1921 - Walter Hagen
1922 - Gene Sarazen
1923 - Gene Sarazen
1924 - Walter Hagen
1925 - Walter Hagen
1926 - Walter Hagen
1927 - Walter Hagen (5)
1928 - Leo Diegel
1929 - Leo Diegel (2)
1930 - Tommy Armour (1)
1931 - Tom Creavy (1)

1932 - Olin Dutra (1)
1933 - Gene Sarazen (3)
1934 - Paul Runyan
1935 - Johnny Revolta (1)
1936 - Denny Shute
1937 - Denny Shute (2)
1938 - Paul Runyan (2)
1939 - Henry Picard (1)
1940 - Byron Nelson
1941 - Vic Ghezzi (1)
1942 - Sam Snead
1943 - No Championship
1944 - Bob Hamilton (1)
1945 - Byron Nelson (2)
1946 - Ben Hogan
1947 - Jim Ferrier (1)
1948 - Ben Hogan (2)
1949 - Sam Snead
1950 - Chandler Harper (1)
1951 - Sam Snead (3)
1952 - Jim Turnesa (1)
1953 - Walter Burkemo (1)
1954 - Chick Harbert (1)
1955 - Doug Ford (1)
1956 - Jack Burke (1)
1957 - Lionel Hebert (1)

Thirty-nine PGA Championships were conducted at match play between 1916 and 1957, and 25 different champions were crowned. Although none of the match play champions succeeded in winning the tournament after it was changed to medal play, the Hebert brothers combined to conquer each of the distinctive formats when Jay Hebert won the 1960 championship three years after Lionel had won the final championship determined by match play. Traditionalists still yearn for a major championship conducted at match play and the debate will rage forever as to whether Palmer and Watson could have won an elusive PGA Championship if the format had never been altered.

*(n) = final victory total for each champion

Dates of Birth

Logically speaking:

> All birthdays are happy.
> All golfers have birthdays.
> Therefore
> All golfers are happy.

Here is a list of golfers and their birthdays.

1. Marty Furgol; January 5, 1918
2. Cary Middlecoff; January 6, 1921
3. Paul Azinger; January 6, 1960
4. Ben Crenshaw; January 11, 1952
5. Jack Nicklaus; January 21, 1940
6. Nick Price; January 28, 1957
7. Curtis Strange; January 30, 1955
8. Payne Stewart; January 30, 1957
9. Jacky Cupit; February 1, 1938
10. Stan Leonard; February 2, 1915
11. Tommy Jacobs; February 13, 1935
12. Bob Goalby; March 14, 1931
13. Bob Charles; March 14, 1936
14. Gay Brewer; March 19, 1932
15. Tommy Bolt; March 31, 1918
16. Phil Rodger; April 3, 1938
17. Bobby Nichols; April 14, 1936
18. Jim Dent; May 9, 1939
19. Mike Souchak; May 10, 1927
20. Ken Venturi; May 15, 1931
21. Sam Snead; May 27, 1912
22. Charles Sifford; June 2, 1922
23. Jim Ferree; June 10, 1931
24. Phil Mickelson; June 16, 1970
25. Billy Casper; June 24, 1931
26. Roger Maltbie; June 30, 1951
27. Moe Norman; July 10, 1929
28. Rocco Mediate; July 17, 1962
29. Gene Littler; July 21, 1930
30. Doug Ford; August 6, 1922
31. Ben Hogan; August 13, 1912
32. Al Geiberger; September 1, 1937
33. Ray Floyd; September 4, 1942
34. Arnold Palmer; September 10, 1929

35. Kermit Zarley; September 29, 1941
36. George Archer; October 1, 1939
37. Fred Couples; October 3, 1959
38. Tommy Armour III; October 8, 1959
39. Bruce Fleisher; October 16, 1948
40. Juan Rodriguez; October 23, 1935
41. Gary Player; November 1, 1935
42. Jack Fleck; November 8, 1921
43. David Duval; November 9, 1971
44. Don January; November 20, 1929
45. Art Wall, Jr.; November 25, 1923
46. Jay Haas; December 2, 1953
47. Lanny Wadkins; December 5, 1949
48. Tiger Woods; December 30, 1975

A Few More Birthdays

1. January: Donna Caponi (1-29-45)
2. February: Patty Berg (2-13-18)
3. March: Hollis Stacey (3-16-54)
4. April: Dale Eggling (4-21-54)
5. May: Laura Baugh (5-31-55)
6. June: Juli Inkster (6-24-60)
7. July: Dina Ammaccapane (7-11-68)
8. August: Dottie Pepper (8-17-65)
9. September: Kathy Whitworth (9-27-39)
10. October: Annika Sorenstam (10-9-70)
11. November: Danielle Ammaccapane (11-27-65)
12. December: Karrie Webb (12-21-74)

Myrtle Beach Golf Courses/1928-1977)

1928 - Pine Lakes International CC, originally Ocean Forest CC
1948 - Dunes Golf and Beach Club
1960 - Surf Golf and Beach Club
1966 - Myrtlewood Golf Course (36 holes)
1966 - Litchfield CC
1967 - Quail Creek GC
1968 - Beachwood GC
1968 - Robbers Roost GC
1968 - Possum Trot GC
1971 - Azalea Sands GC

1971 - Eagle Nest GC
1971 - Cypress Bay GC
1972 - Bay Tree Golf Plantation (54 holes)
1973 - Myrtle Beach National GC (54 holes)
1974 - Arcadian Shores GC
1975 - Waterway Hills GC (27 holes), originally Arcadian Skyway GC
1976 - Deer Track Golf and Country Club (North)
1975 - Carolina Shores GC
1976 - Raccoon Run GC
1977 - Wedgefield Plantation

Five Degrees of Trying Too Hard in Golf
1. Trying to hit the ball
2. Trying to hit the ball up into the air.
3. Trying to hit the ball far.
4. Trying to hit the ball straight.
5. Trying to hit the ball "right."
—from *The Inner Game of Golf* by W. Timothy Gallwey

Canadian Golf Hall of Fame
1. R. Keith Alexander
2. Allan George Balding
3. David L. Black
4. Kenneth Black
5. Gayle Hitchens Borthwick
6. Jocelyne Bourassa
7. Gordon Brydson
8. Dorothy Campbell Hurd Howe
9. Donald Day Carrick, O.B.E.
10. Betty Stanhope Cole
11. Geoffrey Cornish
12. Gary Cowan
13. George Cummings
14. Marion Doherty
15. Phil Farley
16. Pat Fletcher
17. R. Bruce Forbes
18. Alexa Stirling Fraser
19. Richard H. Grimm
20. Florence Harvey
21. Jules Huot

22. Karl Keffer
23. George Knudson
24. William Lamb
25. Stan Leonard
26. George Seymour Lyon
27. Ada MacKenzie
28. Henry Martell
29. Fritz R. Martin
30. Roderick Hugh McIsaac
31. Gail Harvey Moore
32. Albert H. Murray
33. Jack Nicklaus
34. Moe Norman
35. Claude Pattemore
36. Sandra Post
37. Ralph H. Reville
38. Doug Roxburgh
39. Cathy Sherk
40. Douglas Howard Silverberg
41. C. Ross Somerville
42. John B. Steel
43. Marlene Stewart Streit
44. Violet Pooley Sweeny
45. Gordon B. Taylor
46. Stanley Thompson
47. Margaret Todd
48. Nick Weslock
49. Robert Wylie

The Canadian Golf Hall of Fame recognizes extraordinary contributions to Canadian golf. Honored members include professional and amateur golfers and builders of the sport. The Hall of Fame is located at Glen Abbey Golf Club in Oakville, Ontario.

12 Days of Christmas
On the twelfth day of Christmas my true love gave to me...
12 drivers driving
11 divots flying
10 balls a' soaring
9 putters putting
8 carts a' cruising

7 trophies gleaming
6 greens awaiting
5 golden tees
4 argyle socks
3 golf bags
2 pairs of shoes
and an eagle on a par three!

—"A Golfer's Christmas," USGA Christmas card

Corey Pavin's Shotmaking/Table of Contents

1. Foreword by Tom Watson
2. Introduction—-Shotmaking: Part Science, Part Art
3. Chapter 1 - Revisiting the '95 U.S. Open
4. Chapter 2 - Square One: Finding Your Fundamentals
5. Chapter 3 - A 'Working' Tee Shot
6. Chapter 4 - Shaping Your Fairway Woods
7. Chapter 5 - The Iron Man
8. Chapter 6 - Zeroing in with Short Irons
9. Chapter 7 - Wedge Wizardry
10. Chapter 8 - Pitching Like a Pro
11. Chapter 9 - Chipping with Precision
12. Chapter 10 - Working Miracles from Sand
13. Chapter 11 - Putting Is Shotmaking, Too
14. Chapter 12 - Great Escapes
15. Chapter 13 - A Perfect Frame of Mind

Marsh Harbour Golf Links/ Course Description

The unsurpassed beauty of the marshlands and a challenging course equal an unforgettable golfing experience at Marsh Harbour. The Dan Maple/Larry Young designed layout takes you over salt marshes, down fairways edged with pines and through groves of oaks and dogwoods. Located in Calabash, North Carolina, Marsh Harbour is unique in the fact you play in two states in one round. The first nine holes are played in North Carolina and the second nine holes are played in South Carolina. A brief description of each of the eighteen memorable holes is a tantalizing introduction to this great course.

FRONT NINE

1. Opening hole. This hole appears to be a slight dogleg to the right   but it's actually a very sharp dogleg. Placement of the tee shot on this par 4 is a must. The green is well-bunkered and very undulating.

2. The second hole is a slightly downhill par 4 with trees lining both sides of the fairway. Placement of the tee shot is essential and the second shot is played to a two-tiered green.
3. On this straight away hole, length is important off the tee. The long hitter may chance reaching this well-bunkered shallow green in two shots, but the better shot is laying up on the right side of the fairway, leaving a short pitch to this par 5.
4. The longest par 3 on the course has a large accommodating green. The large bunkers guarding the right side of the green must be avoided at all costs.
5. The par 4 fifth hole demands an accurate drive to avoid the sand bunkers on the right and a tree on the left. A well-positioned drive yields a short iron approach to a well-bunkered green.
6. Bunkers, which guard the front and backside of the green, make this par 3 a good test of golf. Landing close to the pin is imperative because of the difficult two-tiered green.
7. From an elevated teeing area of this par 4 the player can see the trouble that lies ahead. Placement of the tee shot on the right side of the fairway leaves a medium iron shot to a slightly uphill well-bunkered green.
8. The intracoastal waterway is a backdrop for one of the most picturesque holes on the course. This long par 3 plays into the prevailing wind which makes club selection a critical consideration.
9. Marshland borders the left side of this par 5. Favor the right side on the tee shot and the left side on the second shot. This will set up a tricky pitch shot to the narrowest green on the course.

BACK NINE

10. The easy appearance is deceptive; this is a difficult driving hole. The tee shot must be down the right side of the fairway in order to have an open approach to the green.
11. The green of this par 3 is carved into a hill with a pond in front and a deep bunker on the left. Proper club selection and pinpoint accuracy will be rewarded.
12. This par 5 requires an accurate drive to avoid the fairway bunker on the right. Lay-up the second shot on the right side leaving a short pitch to a well-bunkered green.
13. Split the fairway with the tee shot to set up a long to medium iron to a three-tiered green.
14. The green of this innocent-looking par 3 is much bigger than it appears from the tee. Avoid being long if possible.
15. A draw played at the fairway bunker will set up a medium iron for the second shot on this dogleg to the left par 4. The second shot is downhill

to a kidney-shaped green.

16. Because it plays uphill, this most demanding par 4 plays longer than the yardage indicates. A good drive should favor the right side to avoid the fairway bunkers. The elevated green has deep bunkers on the right.

17. The signature hole at Marsh Harbour has been labeled as "the challenge of a lifetime." This par 5 hole is divided by marsh into three distinct landing areas. The prevailing wind is in the player's face. Be sure to pick the right club.

18. This great finishing hole requires an accurate tee shot. Don't be fooled by the lack of distance. The second shot over water to a narrow green is a true test of skill.

Metric Golf

If the U.S. citizenry were not intolerant of simple, practical measuring systems, the distances from the regulation (white) tees at Marsh Harbour would look like this:

1	297m
2	292m
3	434m
4	174m
5	302m
6	160m
7	330m
8	156m
9	466m
OUT	2611m
10	334m
11	142m
12	434m
13	334m
14	165m
15	352m
16	367m
17	467m
18	284m
IN	2879m
TOT	5490m

From this enlightened worldly perspective, a typical tee shot by Tiger Woods travels 274 meters instead of 300 yards. Suddenly, traditional championship courses are less vulnerable to modern technology. Note: To assure accuracy, golf course measurements must be established in the shade. Your local meteorologist can validate the importance of this practice.

More Metrics
Metric conversions for outstanding championship sites:

1. Pine Valley, Clementon, NJ   18/70 – 6,190m
2. Bethpage Park (Black), Farmingdale, NY   18/71 – 6,464m
3. Winged Foot (West), Mamaroneck, NY   18/72 – 6,365m
4. Firestone (South), Akron, OH   18/70 – 6,563m
5. Southern Hills, Tulsa, OK   18/71 – 6,439m
6. Wannamoisett, Rumford, RI   18/69 – 6,067m
7. Medinah (No. 3), Medinah, IL   18/72 – 6,739m
8. Bay Hill, Orlando, FL   18/72 – 6,594m
9. Cog Hill (No. 4), Lemont, IL   18/72 – 6,383m
10. Pasatiempo, Santa Cruz, CA   18/72 – 6,210m
11. Cape Breton Highlands, Ingonish, NS   18/72 – 6,032m
12. Maidstone, East Hampton, NY   18/72 – 5,787m
13. East Lake, Atlanta, GA   18/72 – 6,504m
14. Cherry Hills, Englewood, CO   18/72 – 6,640m
15. Plainfield, Plainfield, NJ   18/72 – 6,276m
16. Merion (East), Ardmore, PA   18/70 – 5,931m
17. Royal Birkdale, Southport, England   18/73 – 6,405m
18. Prairie Dunes, Hutchinson, KS   18/70 – 5,986m

It is exceedingly noteworthy that the metric hole is an inviting 10.8 centimeters in width instead of the myopic 4 1/2 inch cylinder that shatters the ego of the golfing proletariat. Metric golf is surely a rewarding and liberating experience!

Welcome to Persimmon Hill GC
PLEASE OBSERVE OUR RULES

1. Please check in before beginning play
2. Shirts and appropriate dress at all times
3. No carts on tees and greens
4. No range balls on course
5. Allow faster players through
6. Rake all sand traps
7. Place all trash in containers

8. Do not damage greens
9. Do not cross fences around course

Scorecards at most courses ask that you adhere to their rules. The rules at Persimmon Hill Golf Club in Tampa, Florida are practical and succinct.

Welcome to Southern Dunes
1. Ante Up
2. Texas Dolly
3. Beauty and the Beast
4. Slingshot
5. Double Trouble
6. Binion's Bluff
7. Deadman's Curve
8. Heaven's Gate
9. Press 'Em Up
10. Dewey's Double Down
11. Dew or Die
12. Dealer's Choice
13. Take It to the Bank
14. Bunkers by the Dozen
15. Go For Broke
16. The Hawk Walk
17. Donley's Ridge
18. Choke Alley

Although none of the holes at Southern Dunes in Haines City, Florida, has attained the mythical memorability of The Road Hole at St. Andrews, each hole has a distinct nomenclature.

A Glossary of Equipment Terminology
1. Bounce — The degree that the sole of a clubhead angles downward from leading edge to trailing edge.
2. Bulge — Curvature of the clubface from heel to toe which is deliberately built into woods so that off-center hits are more playable contingent upon the resulting "gear effect."
3. Cambered sole — Curved sole on an iron from leading edge to back or from heel to toe.
4. Center of gravity — Point inside the clubhead at which its weight is concentrated.

5. Coefficient of restitution — A measure of the elastic properties of a golf ball.

6. Composite — Any clubhead or shaft made of more than one non-metallic material.

7. Face progression — Looking down at a wood clubface at address, the distance from the center of the shaft to the forwardmost point of the clubface.

8. Flange — Protrusion of the back and/or sole of a clubhead, usually an iron or putter.

9. Forged irons — Iron clubheads produced by placing a metal bar between two halves of a die and hammering under pressure into the shape of an iron clubhead.

10. Frequency matched — A constant progression of frequencies (the number of oscillations of a vibrating club) throughout a set of clubs.

11. Game-improvement club — Broad term used to describe clubs that are "forgiving," or produce satisfactory results on mis-hits.

12. Gear effect — The impact from a ball striking the toe of a wood club causes the clubhead, rotating about its center of gravity, to open slightly. The ball reacts by spinning counterclockwise toward the center of the clubface, which results in a right-to-left ball flight. The reverse occurs when a ball strikes the heel of a wood club.

13. Gooseneck — A curvature in the shaft of a putter near the point where it joins the clubhead.

14. Investment casting — A method of manufacturing clubheads. A wax model of the desired head is formed and then surrounded by a ceramic material. The assembly is baked, hardening the ceramic material while the wax melts and drains away. A cavity in the shape of the clubhead is left within the ceramic mold. Molten metal is poured into the cavity and allowed to cool. The ceramic material is then broken away, leaving the investment cast clubhead. (The preceding explanation will hopefully squelch the persistent rumor that investment casting somehow involves an activity performed by a Wall Street broker with a rod and reel, tacklebox and waders).

15. Kick point — Point on the shaft where the maximum amount of flex occurs. The lower the kick point, the higher the ball flies.

16. Lie angle — Angle between the clubshaft and the ground when the clubhead is seated properly at address.

17. Moment of inertia — A measure of the clubhead's resistance to angular acceleration (twisting) during impact. Cavity-back irons will generally have a greater moment of inertia than a blade.

18. Offset — Looking down on the clubhead at address, the distance from the forwardmost point of the hosel to the leading edge of the clubface.

19. Perimeter weighting — Distributing the weight of a clubhead around its periphery.
20. Player's club — An iron whose mass is concentrated mainly in the hitting area, thereby delivering a solid feel on shots struck on the "sweet spot." A "player's club" is relatively "unforgiving" on heel and toe hits.
21. Progressive offset — In a set of irons, the leading edge of a short iron is almost flush with the forwardmost point of the hosel, but each subsequent iron in the set is constructed so that the leading edge is positioned progressively farther back from the hosel.
22. Roll — Curvature of a wood clubface from top to bottom, deliberately built into clubs for cosmetic reasons; if the clubface has no roll it will appear to have little or no loft.
23. Swingweight — A static measure of a club's balance at a point 12 to 14 inches from the grip end. Swing weight describes how heavy the club feels when you swing it, not its actual overall weight.
24. Tipping the shaft — Trimming the clubshaft at the point where it tapers and enters the hosel. The shaft generally becomes stiffer when it is tipped.
25. Torque — Rotational twisting that occurs in the shaft during the swing.

—from *Golf Digest*/March 1992:
"Equipmentspeak: What Does It All Mean?" by Guy Yocum

Western Open/Miscellaneous

1. The Western Open is the second oldest professional tournament in the U.S. Its inaugural championship was held in 1899.
2. The Western Open was conducted at Match Play in 1910 and 1911.
3. Amateur Chick Evans won the Western Open in 1910.
4. Canadian Stan Leonard is the oldest champion in Western history, having won the title in 1960 at age 45.
5. In 1985, Scott Verplank became the first amateur in over thirty years to win a professional tournament when he defeated Jim Thorpe in a sudden death playoff to capture the Western Open.
6. Harry Cooper defeated Ky Laffoon in the only 36 hole playoff in Western Open history to win the title in 1934. Both men were tied at 274 after 72 holes. In the first 18 hole playoff, both players tied again with 67. On the next 18 holes Cooper defeated Laffoon by shooting 66 to Laffoon's 69.
7. The dominant player of the late Thirties, Ralph Guldahl won three consecutive Westerns from 1936 to 1938.
8. The Tournament Record of 268 is held jointly by Sam Snead (1949) and Chi Chi Rodriguez (1964)

Western Open/Multi-Victories

1. Willie Anderson 1902, '04, '08, '09
2. Alex Smith 1903, '06
3. Robert Simpson 1907, '11
4. Macdonald Smith 1912, '25, '33
5. Jim Barnes 1914, '17, '19
6. Walter Hagen 1916, '21, '26, '27, '32
7. Jock Hutchinson 1920, '23
8. Ralph Guldahl 1936, '37, '38
9. Ben Hogan 1946, '48
10. Sam Snead 1949, '50
11. Lloyd Mangrum 1952, '54
12. Arnold Palmer 1961, '63
13. Billy Casper 1965, '66, '69, '73
14. Jack Nicklaus 1967, '68
15. Tom Watson 1974, '77, '84
16. Mark McCumber 1983, '89
17. Nick Price 1993, '94
18. Tiger Woods 1997, '99

The multiple winners of the Western Open constitute a veritable *Who's Who* of professional golf. The caliber of golfers on this list is unmatched by any tournament past or present. The performance in the Western by Willie Anderson and Walter Hagen parallel their achievements in the "legitimate" majors. Anderson is a four time champion of both the U.S. Open and the Western Open. Hagen recorded five victories in both the P.G.A. Championship and the Western Open. Both Hagen and Macdonald Smith triumphed at the Western in three different decades.

Western Open/Geographical Site Distribution (1899–2000)

1. Illinois (53)
2. Ohio (9)
3. Michigan (8)
4. Missouri (5)
5. Wisconsin (4)
6. Tennessee (2)
7. Minnesota (2)
8. Indiana (2)
9. Iowa (2)
10. Arizona (2)
11. California (2)

12. Texas (1)
13. Utah (1)
14. New York (1)
15. Oregon (1)
16. Pennsylvania (1)

Stump your friends with golfing trivia—-What state has never hosted the Western Open: a) Pennsylvania; b) Tennessee; c) Nebraska; d) New York; e) Indiana?

Western Open/Randomly Selected Results

1902 Euclid Club (Euclid, Ohio)

	Player	Total	Money
1	Willie Anderson	299	$150
T2	Willie Smith	304	
T2	W. H. Way	304	
4	Stewart Gardner	310	
5	Laurie Auchterlonie	316	
6	David Bell	319	
7	B. Nichols	321	
8	Alex Smith	322	

1912 Idlewild C.C. (Flossmoor, Illinois)

	Player	Total	Money
1	Macdonald Smith	299	$300
2	Alex Robertson	302	
3	J. J. McDermott	303	
T4	Walter Fovargue	305	
T4	Tom McNamara	305	
6	Gil Nicholls	306	
7	Fred McLeod	310	
8	Robert Simpson	312	

1952 Westwood C.C. (St. Louis, Missouri)

	Player	Total	Money
1	Lloyd Mangrum	274	$2,400
2	Bobby Locke	282	
3	Johnny Palmer	283	
T4	Dow Finsterwald	285	
T4	Dick Mayer	285	
T6	Shelley Mayfield	286	
T6	Ted Kroll	286	

T8	Tommy Bolt	287	
T8	Jack Burke, Jr.	287	
T8	Fred Haas	287	
T8	Jim Turnesa	287	

1962 Medinah C.C. (Medinah, Illinois)

	Player	Total	Money
1	Jacky Cupit	281	$11,000
2	Billy Casper	283	
T3	Fred Hawkins	286	
T4	Gary Player	286	
T5	Julius Boros	287	
T5	Al Geiberger	287	
7	Arnold Palmer	288	
T8	Jim Ferree	291	
T8	Dow Finsterwald	291	
T8	Harold Kneece	291	
T8	Stan Leonard	291	
T8	Jack Nicklaus	291	

1972 Sunset Ridge C.C. (Northfield, Illinois)

	Player	Total	Money
1	Jim Jamieson	271	$30,000
2	Labron Harris, Jr.	277	
T3	Hale Irwin	280	
T3	Bob Lunn	280	
T3	Jim Wiechers	280	
T6	Tommy Aaron	281	
T6	David Graham	281	
T6	Bobby Nichols	281	
T6	J.C. Snead	281	
T6	Tom Weiskopf	281	

1982 Butler National G.C. (Oak Brook, Illinois)

	Player	Total	Money
1	Tom Weiskopf	276	$63,000
2	Larry Nelson	277	
3	Bob Gilder	278	
T4	Bill Rogers	280	
T4	Jim Thorpe	280	
6	Curtis Strange	282	
7	Mark Pfeil	283	

T8	George Burns	284
T8	Tom Jenkins	284
T8	Doug Tewell	284
T8	Lanny Wadkins	284

1992 Cog Hill Golf & C.C. (Lemont, Illinois)

	Player	Total	Money
1	Ben Crenshaw	276	$198,000
2	Greg Norman	277	
T3	Chip Beck	278	
T3	Fred Couples	278	
T3	Blaine McCallister	278	
T3	Duffy Waldorf	278	
T7	Tom Purtzer	279	
T7	Jeff Sluman	279	

Brad Bryant's (Dr. Dirt) Top Ten Alternative Nicknames for Himself

1. Dr. Paydirt
2. Commander-in-Chief of All Dirt Forces
3. Professor Pete Moss
4. Bart's brother
5. Bear (What? Bear Bryant has already been taken?)
6. Alligator (because they lay around and fish all day...and that's my goal)
7. 1995 Walt Disney World/Oldsmobile Classic Champion
8. Armani (NOT)
9. Arnold Ziffel (the pig in "Green Acres")
10. Mr. Clean

—from *Golf Magazine*/February 1996

Number of Golf Courses Per State / 1997

1. Florida – 1,170
   (Is this count correct? Should California demand a recount?)
2. California – 942
3. Michigan – 906
4. New York – 838
5. Texas – 838
6. Ohio – 786
7. Pennsylvania – 709
8. Illinois – 695
9. North Carolina – 563

The state of Florida has more golf courses than Alaska, Delaware, Rhode Island, Wyoming, Vermont, New Mexico, Hawaii, Idaho, Montana, Utah, North Dakota, New Hampshire, South Dakota and Washington, D.C., combined.

—-from *Florida Golfer* / Summer 1998

TOP TEN Ways to Learn the Rules Better

1. Read the Definitions (Section II) in the rulebook to learn, for instance, that a stroke is only the forward movement of the club with the intention of striking the ball.
2. Understand that the course is subdivided into four sections that call for different rules procedures. The sections are (1) teeing grounds, (2) putting greens, (3) hazards and (4) everything else, which is labeled as "through the green."
3. Don't touch a ball in play until you know exactly what to do next.
4. If you are playing that bastardized form of the game known as "winter rules," get the specifics right. How far can the ball be moved? Does the liberalization apply only in the fairways or does it apply "through the green"?
5. Don't play match play and stroke play simultaneously. It won't work under the rules.
6. Read the local rules on the backs of scorecards and often supplemented by notices posted on bulletin boards.
7. In a four-ball match, any player can lift his ball on a putting green, or require that any other ball be lifted.
8. When in dire straits, you can always use the stroke-and-distance penalty option.
9. To avoid playing a "wrong ball" put a distinguishing mark on your ball.
10. A golfer can (and should) repair ball marks and old hole plugs on the putting green—-but nothing else.

—-from Frank Hannigan in *Golf Digest*/March 1992

Why "Winter Rules" are Insidious

1. "Winter rules" destroy more turf than they protect.
2. How often do you get truly bad lies to begin with?
3. Making a habit of "winter rules" will damage your swing, perhaps irreparably. A ball pedestaled atop turf lets you get away with "coming off the ball" and all sorts of other mistakes which creep into your swing, most of which soon become second nature. The damage may not be apparent at first. But then neither is the damage done by a termite.

4. "Winter rules" undermine your whole game, giving you a false sense of well-being. Nobody whose handicap is determined with preferred lies can play to it without them.

5. "Winter rules" lead to all the other improprieties of golf such as hitting second shots (mulligans), conceding yourself putts (gimmes), and picking up following a failed recovery. Every round you play becomes a practice round.

6. You are deprived of that transcendental experience that gives golf its uniqueness. Whatever it is, it can only be found playing the ball as it lies and the course as you find it. Preferred lies subtract from the unexpected and the undeserved, and golf ceases to be the adventure it ought to be.

—from Charles Price in *Golf Digest*/August 1992

13.5 Best Courses in Maine

On a per capita basis, Maine must be considered a golf Mecca, and the venues are excellent. All course measurements are in non-metric equivalents, i.e. yards.

1.	Webhannet GC, Kennebunk, ME	18/72 - 6,200
2.	Bideford-Saco, Saco, ME	18/70 - 6,300
3.	Kebo Valley GC, Bar Harbor, ME	18/70 - 6,200
4.	Gorham CC, Gorham, ME	18/71 - 6,509
5.	Samoset Resort, Rockport, ME	18/70 - 6,352
6.	Sugarloaf GC, Carrabasset Valley, ME	18/72 - 6,922
7.	Sable Oaks GC, South Portland, ME	18/70 - 6.359
8.	Bethel Inn & CC, Bethel, ME	18/72 - 6,663
9.	Penobscot Valley CC, Orono, ME	18/72 - 6,301
10.	Poland Springs GC, Poland Springs, ME	18/71 - 6,172
11.	Aroostook Valley CC, Fort Fairfield, ME	18/72 - 6,304
12.	Mingo Springs GC, Rangeley, ME	18/70 - 6,000
13.5	Bangor Municipal GC, Bangor, ME	27/72/36 - 6,500/3,003

The Modern Grand Slam

As we all know, only five golfers can claim all four of the modern major championships, The Masters, U.S. Open, British Open and P.G.A. Championship, on their resumes.

1. Gene Sarazen, 1935*
2. Ben Hogan, 1953
3. Gary Player, 1965

4. Jack Nicklaus, 1966
5. Tiger Woods, 2000
*year in which final leg of Grand Slam was achieved

The Venerable Slam

Only four golfers have claimed the four historical and prestigious events that I have designated as the "Venerable Slam:" British Open, U.S. Open, Western Open and Canadian Open.

1. Walter Hagen, 1931*
2. Tommy Armour, 1931
3. Arnold Palmer, 1961
4. Tiger Woods, 2000
*year in which final leg of the Venerable Slam was achieved

Heritage Classic: Tournament of Major Champions (1969—2000)

After the initial thirty years of stellar competition, a significant percentage of the winners of the Heritage Classic were owners of at least one major championship. Harbour Town Golf Links is definitely a venue for identifying major champions.

1969 - Arnold Palmer
1970 - Bob Goalby
1971 - Hale Irwin
1972 - Johnny Miller
1973 - Hale Irwin
1974 - Johnny Miller
1975 - Jack Nicklaus
1976 - Hubert Green
1977 - Graham Marsh*
1978 - Hubert Green
1979 - Tom Watson
1980 - Doug Tewell*
1981 - Bill Rogers
1982 - Tom Watson
1983 - Fuzzy Zoeller
1984 - Nick Faldo
1985 - Bernhard Langer
1986 - Fuzzy Zoeller
1987 - Davis Love III

1988 - Greg Norman
1989 - Payne Stewart
1990 - Payne Stewart
1991 - Davis Love III
1992 - Davis Love III
1993 - David Edwards*
1994 - Hale Irwin
1995 - Bob Tway
1996 - Loren Roberts*
1997 - Nick Price
1998 - Davis Love III
1999 - Glen Day*
2000 - Stewart Cink*

*These players have not won a major championship on the PGA Tour as of 01/01/01, however it is noteworthy that both Mr. Marsh and Mr. Tewell have won a major championship on the Senior PGA Tour.

Real Golfers

1. Real golfers don't miss putts; they are "robbed." —John Thomas Trizuto
2. Real golfers don't step on their opponent's ball while looking for it in the rough. —Jack Maloney
3. Real golfers don't use naked-lady tees. —Steve Lindroth
4. Real golfers go to work to relax. —George Dillon
5. Real golfers know how to count over five when they have a bad hole. — Dud Smith
6. Real golfers do not use their putter to get the ball out of the hole.—Dean F. James
7. Real golfers never eat quiche; they eat hot dogs and club sandwiches.— Jess Bragg
8. Real golfers tape The Masters so they can go play themselves.—George W. Roope
9. Real golfers always use a brand new ball on the sixteenth hole at Cypress Point.—Michael Gordon
10. Real golfers never strike a caddie with a driver. The sand wedge is far more effective. —Huxtable Pippey

>   —Quotations from a "Real Golfers"
>   contest held by Pat Sullivan for *The San Francisco Chronicle*

11. Real golfers are not named Huxtable Pippey unless they are characters in a story by P. G. Wodehouse.

Selected Excerpts from Nick Price's "Notes after Reading Sam Snead's Article in Golf Digest, February 1984"

1. People who swing too fast have a tough time coordinating their arms and legs.
2. Think well in advance of what's coming up and ensure you have enough time to do it. People tend to make mistakes when hurried or pushed into things. Always have enough time.
3. Never denounce the game. No single person alive or dead is bigger or better than the wonderful game of golf.
4. Dedication is thinking about the swing and the game even when you're on holiday.

—from *The Swing* by Nick Price

Golf and Tradition

1. Tradition is a game played afoot.
2. It is a game played on the ground as well as in the air.
3. It is turf without uniform color or texture.
4. It is firm and dry fairways.
5. It is putting surfaces maintained at a sensible pace.
6. It is unpredictable bounces of the ball, off slopes gentle and severe, with disheartening results and undeserved success.
7. It is holes that look like they evolved from the terrain.
8. It is strategies that maintain our interest.
9. It is a water hazard provided solely by nature.
10. It is a simple clubhouse with massive showerheads and a modest menu.
11. It is a round that should be accomplished in three hours, not six.
12. It is the absence of cartpaths.
13. It is a game that is affordable for every man and woman.
14. It is the game we'd like to play from now on.

—- from "On Tradition", *Golf Digest*/May 1995

OJT

Although OJT (On-the-Job Training) is often overlooked, it is a powerful way to learn. Many players who became successful professionals were people who, early in life, caddied for someone who were knowledgeable about the game. In other words, they saw the job done right. George Knudson was unequivocally the best ball-striker of his era. As an aspiring young golfer, "the Maestro" spent hours watching golf swings. These fellows (particularly Mr. Hogan) were his teachers.

1. Stan Leonard
2. Al Balding
3. BEN HOGAN
4. Sam Snead
5. Jimmy Demaret
6. Jackie Burke
7. Lionel Hebert
8. Jay Hebert
9. Dick Mayer
10. Tommy Bolt
11. Ted Kroll
12. Julius Boros
13. Lloyd Mangrum
14. Cary Middlecoff
15. Ken Venturi
16. Billy Maxwell
17. Gene Littler
18. Art Wall
19. Don January

"He had a million-dollar swing and a ten-cent putter."
—-Jack Nicklaus describing George Knudson

Wimbledon: Men's Champions of the 20th Century

With apologies to the Champions at Wimbledon in the 19th century, especially Williams Renshaw who claimed the Championship 7 times in the 1880s, allow me to list the 48 illustrious competitors who have won the Wimbledon tournament in the 20th century. Among major professional sporting contests, only golf and Wimbledon tennis routinely stage their championships on a grass surface. Baseball and football aficionados are undeniably envious of this stalwart traditionalism.

1. Arthur Gore; 1901, '08, '09
2. Laurie Doherty; 1902, '03, '04, '05, '06
3. Norman Brookes; 1907, '14
4. Anthony Wilding; 1910, '11, '12, '13
5. Gerald Patterson; 1919, '22
6. Bill Tilden; 1920, '21, '30
7. William Johnston; 1923
8. Jean Borotra; 1924, '26
9. Rene Lacoste; 1925, '28

71

10. Henri Cochet; 1927, '29
11. Sidney Wood; 1931
12. Ellsworth Vines; 1932
13. Jack Crawford; 1933
14. Fred Perry; 1934, '35, '36
15. Don Budge; 1937, '38
16. Bobby Riggs; 1939
17. Yvon Petra; 1946
18. Jack Kramer; 1947
19. Bob Falkenburg; 1948
20. Ted Schroeder; 1949
21. Budge Patty; 1950
22. Dick Savitt; 1951
23. Frank Sedgman; 1952
24. Vic Sexias; 1953
25. Jaroslav Drobny; 1954
26. Tony Trabert; 1955
27. Lew Hoad; 1956, '57
28. Ashley Cooper; 1958
29. Alex Olmedo; 1959
30. Neale Fraser; 1960
31. Rod Laver; 1961, '62, '68, '69
32. Chuck McKinley; 1963
33. Roy Emerson; 1964, '65
33. Roy Emerson; 1964; '65
34. Manuel Santana; 1966
35. John Newcombe; 1967; '71
36. Jan Kodes; 1970, '73
37. Stan Smith; 1972
38. Jimmy Conners; 1974, '82
39. Arthur Ashe; 1975
40. Bjorn Borg; 1976, '77, '78, '79, '80
41. John McEnroe; 1981, '83, '84
42. Boris Becker; 1985, '86, '89
43. Pat Cash; 1987
44. Stefan Edberg; 1988, '90
45. Michael Stich; 1991
46. Andre Agassi; 1992, '99
47. Pete Sampras; 1993, '94, '95, '97, '98, '00
48. Richard Krajicek; 1996

Fraternity Golf

An incomplete list of heroic golfers from the Homeric epics, *The Great Big Iliad* and *The Odyssey Putter*.

1. ΑΡΝΟΛΔ ΠΑΛΜΕΡ
2. ΣΑΜ ΣΝΕΑΔ
3. ΩΑΛΤΕΡ ΗΑΓΕΝ
4. ϑΟΗΝΝΨ ΜΙΛΛΕΡ
5. ΑΛ ΓΕΙΒΕΡΓΕΡ
6. ΤΟΝΨ ΛΕΜΑ
7. ΠΑΥΛ ΑΖΙΝΓΕΡ
8. ΓΑΡΨ ΠΛΑΨΕΡ
9. ΠΑΥΛ ΡΥΝΨΑΝ
10. ΧΡΑΙΓ ΣΤΑΔΛΕΡ

Sorority Sisters

Εθυαλ τιμε φορ ηεροιχ Γρεεκ γολφερσ οφ της φεμινινε γενδερ.*

1. ΑΝΝΙΚΑ ΣΟΡΕΝΣΤΑΜ
2. ΒΑΒΕ ΖΑΗΑΡΙΑΣ
3. ΗΟΛΛΙΣ ΣΤΑΧΨ
4. ΔΟΤΤΙΕ ΠΕΠΠΕΡ
5. ΜΙΧΚΕΨ ΩΡΙΓΗΤ
6. ΛΑΥΡΑ ΒΑΥΓΗ
7. ΠΑΤΤΨ ΒΕΡΓ
8. ϑΥΔΨ ΡΑΝΚΙΝ
9. ΜΥΦΦΙΝ ΣΠΕΝΧΕΡ–ΔΕςΛΙΝ
10. ΣΥΣΙΕ ΒΕΡΝΙΝΓ

*Equal time for heroic Greek golfers of the feminine gender.

Harvey Penick's Favorite Swings

1. Macdonald Smith
2. Ben Crenshaw
3. Mickey Wright
4. Dave Marr
5. Al Geiberger

8 Traits of Champion Golfers
One. Focus
Two. Abstract Thinking
Three. Emotional Stability
Four. Dominance
Five. Tough-Mindedness
Six. Confidence
Seven. Self-Sufficiency
Eight. Optimum Arousal

—from *8 Traits of Champion Golfers* by Graham and Stabler

Lee Eisenberg's 9 Fairways of Hell
1. Ambition
2. Impatience
3. Frustration
4. Overanalysis
5. Gullibility
6. Self-Deception
7. The Klutz Factor
8. Tightness
9. Desperation: Nine tortuous fairways that inevitably lead to
10. **Discovery**

There is no magical or mysterious secret—just self-discovery which makes the whole journey worthwhile.

—-from *Breaking Eighty* by Lee Eisenberg

Gary Player's Worldwide Professional Victories
Like the *Energizer* bunny, Mr. Player keeps going…and going…and going…

1. East Rand Open, 1955
2. Egyptian Match-play, 1955
3. South African PGA Challenge, 1955
4. East Rand Open, 1956
5. South African Open, 1956
6. Dunlop Tournament, 1956
7. Ampol, 1956
8. Australian PGA, 1957
9. Coughs Harbour, 1957
10. Transvaal Open, 1957

11. Kentucky Derby Open, 1958
12. Natal Open, 1958
13. Australian Open, 1958
14. Ampol, 1958
15. Coughs Harbour, 1958
16. British Open, 1959
17. Transvaal Open, 1959
18. South African PGA, 1959
19. Natal Open, 1959
20. Western Province Open, 1959
21. Dunlop Open, 1959
22. Victoria Open, 195923.
23. South African Open, 1960
24. South African PGA, 1960
25. Dunlop Masters, 1960
26. Transvaal Open, 1960
27. Natal Open, 1960
28. Western Province Open, 1960
29. Masters, 1961
30. Lucky International Open, 1961
31. Sunshine, 1961
32. Yomiuri Open, 1961
33. Ampol, 1961
34. PGA Championship, 1962
35. Transvaal Open, 1962
36. Natal Open, 1962
37. Australian Open, 1962
38. San Diego Open, 1963
39. Sponsored 5000, 1963
40. Transvaal Open, 1963
41. Liquid Air, 1963
42. Richelieu Grand Prix Capetown, 1963
43. Richelieu Grand Prix Johannesburg, 1963
44. Dunlop Masters, 1963
45. Australian Open, 1963
46. 500 Festival, 1964
47. Pensacola Open, 1964
48. Dunlop Masters, 1964
49. U.S. Open, 1965
50. South African Open, 1965
51. World Series, 1965
52. World Match Play, 1965

53. NTL Challenge Cup, 1965
54. World Cup (Individual), 1965
55. Australian Open, 1965
56. South African Open, 1966
57. Natal Open, 1966
58. Transvaal Open, 1966
59. World Match Play, 1966
60. Dunlop Masters, 1967
61. South African Open, 1967
62. British Open, 1968
63. South African Open, 1968
64. Natal Open, 1968
65. Western Province Open, 1968
66. World Series, 1968
67. World Match Play, 1968
68. Australian Wills Masters, 1968
69. Tournament of Champions, 1969
70. South African Open, 1969
71. South African PGA, 1969
72. Australian Open, 1969
73. Australian Wills Masters, 1969
74. Greater Greensboro Open, 1970
75. Australian Open, 1970
76. Dunlop International, 1970
77. Greater Jacksonville Open, 1971
78. National Airlines Open, 1971
79. General Motors Open, 1971
80. Western Province Open, 1971
81. Dunlop Masters, 1971
82. World Match Play, 1971
83. PGA Championship, 1972
84. Greater New Orleans Open, 1972
85. Dunlop Masters, 1972
86. South African Open, 1972
87. Western Province Open, 1972
88. World Series, 1972
89. Japan Airlines Open, 1972
90. Brazilian Open, 1972
91 Southern Open, 1973
92. General Motors Open, 1973
93. World Match Play, 1973
94. Masters, 1974

95. British Open, 1974
96. Danny Thomas-Memphis Classic, 1974
97. Dunlop Masters, 1974
98. Rand International, 1974
99. General Motors Open, 1974
100. Ibergolf Tournament, 1974
101. La Manag Tiurnament, 1974
102. Australian Open, 1974
103. Brazilian Open, 1974
104. South African Open, 1975
105. General Motors Classic, 1975
106. Lancome Trophy, 1975
107. Dunlop Masters, 1976
108. South African Open, 1976
109. General Motors Open, 1976
110. South African Open, 1977
111. ICL Transvaal, 1977
112. World Cup (Individual), 1977
113. Masters, 1978
114. Tournament of Champions, 1978
115. Houston Open, 1978
116. South African Open, 1979
117. South African PGA, 1979
118. Kronenbrau Masters, 1979
119. Sun City, 1979
120. Trophee Boigny, 1980
121. Chilean Open, 1980
122. South African Open, 1981
123. South African PGA, 1981
124. U.S. Skins Game, 1983
125. Johnnie Walker, 1984
126. Quadel Seniors Classic, 1985
127. PGA Seniors Championship, 1986
128. United Hospital Classic, 1986
129. Denver Post Champions, 1986
130. Nissan Senior Skins, 1986
131. U.S. Senior Open, 1987
132. Mazda Senior TPC, 1987
133. Paine Webber World Senior Invitational, 1987
134. Northville Invitational, 1987
135. U.S. Senior Open, 1988
136. PGA Senior Championship, 1988

137. Aetna Challenge, 1988
138. Southwestern Bell Classic, 1988
139. GTE North Classic, 1988
140. British Senior Open, 1988
141. Nissan Senior Skins, 1988
142. GTE North Classic, 1989
143. RJR Championship, 1989
144. British Senior Open ,1989
145. PGA Senior Championship, 1990
146. British Senior Open, 1990
147. Royal Caribbean Classic, 1991
148. Nissan Senior Skins, 1991
149. Bank One Classic, 1993
150. Irish Senior Open, 1993
151. Skills Challenge, 1994
152. Bank One Classic, 1995
153. Bank of Boston Classic, 1995
154. Bank One Classic, 1996
155. Wentworth Masters, 1997
156. Senior British Open, 1997
157. Dai Ichi Semei Cup, 1997
158. Northville Long Island Classic, 1998
159. Senior Skins Game, 2000

No one will be surprised——least of all Gary Player——-when he wins a tournament somewhere on the globe in the new millennium. Player remains an indomitable combination of optimism and persistence.

New Orleans Open/Multiple Champions
1. Henry Picard; 1939, '41
2. Byron Nelson; 1945, '46
3. Billy Casper; 1958, '75
4. Bo Wininger; 1962, '63
5. Frank Beard; 1966, '71
6. Tom Watson; 1980, '81
7. Ben Crenshaw; 1987, '94
8. Chip Beck; 1988, '92
9. Carlos Franco; 1999, 2000

First played in 1938, winners of the New Orleans Open include Jimmy Demaret, Jack Nicklaus, Lee Trevino and Gary Player...plus the aforementioned 9 two time champions. No golfer has been able to claim an elusive third victory in New Orleans. Billy Casper's victory in 1975 was his 51st and final PGA Tour title.

.

Golfactoids

1. A compilation of random, nevertheless amazing facts.
2. Doug Ford finished among the top-10 money winners on the PGA Tour each year during the decade of the '50s.
3. Calvin Peete ranked first in the statistical category for Driving Accuracy on the PGA Tour each year in the decade of the '80s.
4. Each time that Curtis Strange was the leading money winner on the PGA Tour, he established a new standard (1985-$542,321; 1987-$925,941;1988-$1,147,644).
5. Roberto de Vicenzo has more than 200 victories worldwide.
6. In 1959 Ben Hogan won his fifth Colonial National Invitational. It was Hogan's 63rd and final victory on the PGA Tour.
7. In 1965 Sam Snead captured the Greater Greensboro Open at the age of 52 years and 10 months. It was his eighth triumph in the Greensboro tournament.
8. Bob Charles became the first lefthanded winner on the PGA Tour at the 1963 Houston Classic.
9. The first Ryder Cup matches were played in 1927 at Worcester C.C.in Worcester, Massachusetts. The United States defeated Great Britain 9_ to 2_. Tommy Armour played for Great Britain in 1927. He is the only golfer to represent the U.S. and Great Britain in the Ryder Cup competition.
10. Fuzzy Zoeller is the only player to win the Masters in his first appearance.
11. Sam Snead and Raymond Floyd are the only golfers to win PGA tournaments in four different decades.
12. Gary Player is the only player to claim the British Open in three different decades.
13. Ellsworth Vines and Frank Conner are the only two men to have played in the U.S. Open in tennis and golf.

Tucson Open/Multiple Winners

1. Jimmy Demaret; 1946, '47
2. Lloyd Mangrum; 1949, '50
3. Tommy Bolt; 1953, '55
4. Don January; 1960, '63

5. Lee Trevino; 1969, '70
6. Johnny Miller; 1974, '75, '76, '81
7. Bruce Lietzke; 1977, '79
8. Tom Watson; 1978, '84
9. Jim Thorpe; 1985, '86
10. Phil Mickelson; 1991; '95, '96

1982 PGA Tour Qualifying Tournament Results

In November 1982, fifty players earned their 1983 Tour Cards by surviving six grueling rounds of competition at Sawgrass G.C. and the Tournament Players Club in Ponte Vedra Beach, Florida.

1.	Donnie Hammond	419
2.	David Peoples	433
3.	Nick Price	435
4.	Mac O'Grady	436
5.	Tze Chung-chen	436
6.	Buddy Gardner	436
7.	Bob Boyd	436
8.	Richard Zokol	436
9.	Dan Forsman	437
10.	Gary McCord	437
11.	John McComish	437
12.	Mike Peck	438
13.	Tom Jones	438
14.	Joey Rassett	439
15.	Ken Green	439
16.	Jeff Sanders	439
17.	Bill Sander	439
18.	Rod Nuckolls	440
19.	Lindy Miller	440
20.	Steve Hart	440
21.	Mike Brannan	440
22.	Mick Soli	441
23.	Lyn Lott	441
24.	Doug Black	441
25.	Curt Byrum	441
26.	Larry Rinker	441
27.	David Ogrin	442
28.	Ivan Smith	442
29.	Russ Cochran	442

30. Jimmy Roy	443
31. Bill Murchison	443
32. Loren Roberts	443
33. Tony Sills	443
34. Darrell Kestner	443
35. Wally Armstrong	443
36. Mike Gove	444
37. Ray Stewart	444
38. Mark Coward	444
39. Ronnie Black	444
40. Lonnie Nielsen	444
41. Blaine McCallister	444
42. Tom Lehman	444
43. Rafael Alarcon	444
44. Lars Meyerson	445
45. Jon Chaffee	446
46. Rick Pearson	446
47. Rick Dalpos	446
48. Sammy Rachels	446
49. Ken Kelley	446
50. Jeff Sluman	446

ATTENTION: John Feinstein. The preceding list of players would provide excellent journalistic fodder for a "whatever happened to" omnibus.

Happy Golfing!

V. DeBunkering Golf's Myths

> WARNING: Information contained in the subse-
> quent pages could adversely affect the causality
> matrix in the golfing lobe of your brain.

The modern golfer inhabits a quagmire infested with confusing technical data, contradictory instructional theory, and a plethora of misleading and
misunderstood information. By comprehending some of golf's hoariest
myths, the player is furnished with the insight to accomplish the primary
objective in every round of golf: survival. "Survival" means returning to the
course another day to face the sustaining reassurance of golf's madness.
Golfers aspire to return to the scene and play it again and again.

Driving Myths

"What other people may find in poetry
or art museums,
I find in the flight of a good drive."

—Arnold Palmer

Critics of golf opine the incongruity of a game in which a 300 yard drive
and a three foot putt both count one stroke. Surely a 300 yard drive is a
greater feat than holing a three foot putt. I would contend that the fragile
juxtaposition of the powerful drive and the delicate putt is one of the primary
fascinations of the game. Moreover, physical stature in the game of golf is not
intimately linked to the ability to drive the ball.

The art of driving the golf ball has been unjustly maligned for years. Every
golfer has heard such preposterous and tired bromides as "Drive for show; putt
for dough," or "It's not how you drive, it's how you arrive." Avuncular Harvey
Penick made a comparably erroneous observation: "A man who can putt is a
match for anyone; a man who can't putt is a match for no one."

Legendary champions of the game (and Marshall Smith) acknowledge that driving is the foundation of great golf:

1. "The man who drives the longer ball has the rest of the game made easier and more certain. There is no stroke in golf that gives the same amount of pleasure as does the perfect driving of the ball from the tee, none that makes the heart feel lighter, and none that seems to bring the glow of delight into the watching eye as this one does." —Harry Vardon

2. "Long driving is of prime importance in golf. It need not be long enough to make the world gasp. But it must be long enough to give the golfer some chance against par, and to put him on good terms with himself." —Ted Ray

3. "There is no doubt that the short game is critical to scoring. But you will wear yourself down eventually if you have to chip and putt to play well all the time. To me the highest pleasure in the game is in learning a swing that will keep the ball in play."—Nick Price

4. "I work on having the same smooth tempo with my driver as I do with all my clubs, and I never rush my backswing. I focus on getting the ball in the middle of the fairway; to me, the tee shot is the most important one because it sets up the rest of the hole."—Nancy Lopez

5. "(P)laying golf is like painting…When you stand on the tee box and look down the fairway, you're staring at a blank canvas. The drive is going to be the first—and boldest—stroke you're going to paint on the hole…When you're driving the ball well, you swing with confidence and leave yourself high-percentage approach shots onto the greens…(Your driver) is the biggest weapon in your bag, and to play your best golf you have to able to use it."—Marshall Smith

6. "I consider the driver the most important club in the bag…Good driving affects all facets of your game. If you can swing the longest club with rhythm and tempo, chances are you'll do the same with the shorter clubs. Good driving leaves shorter approach shots to par-4's and creates opportunities to attack par-5's."—Kathy Whitworth

7. "Placing the ball off the tee into a position from where the next shot can be hit unencumbered is THE most fundamental factor in consistent play. Playing from the fairway starts a very desirable chain reaction. The biggest disaster shots in the game are usually tee shots. Once you're on

or near the fairway, you're far less likely to make a big mistake on the hole. In sum, being in play off the tee simply make the game easier." — Ray Floyd

Good driving is the cornerstone of good golf and a good drive from the first tee is the key to good driving. A good drive on the first tee sets the tone for the entire round. It relieves tension and stimulates confidence. Here are some pragmatic guidelines for that inaugural shot of the round.

1. Warm up.
2. Don't rush.
3. Select the club that will find the fairway.
4. Focus on your target (where not how).
5. Complete your backswing.
6. Don't steer the ball.
7. Keep your balance.

Enjoy your drive. Recognize what your psyche has always known. Driving is the essence of golf. It's why we play the game.

Putting Myths

> "Love and putting are mysteries for the philosopher to solve. Both subjects are beyond golfers."
> —Tommy Armour

The notion that putting supremacy means golfing supremacy is the most damnable myth in golf. Golf is an infinite series of shotmaking opportunities. All shotmaking opportunities are equally important. Each shot played counts a single stroke. Since most golfers are indoctrinated with the notion that putting is the key to success, they overemphasize the outcome of their putting results. When the inevitable missed putt occurs, the necessity to avoid additional misses creates tension and paralysis. The die is cast and the unwitting golfer stamps out a series of missed putts.

The golfer who realizes that a putt is merely one more shotmaking opportunity understands the true essence of the game: play the shots within your capabilities and accept the results. Jack Burke, a truly great putter from a past era, says that putting is like rolling a ball with your hand except you're using a stick. The objective is to roll the ball. Do not stroke the ball. Do not hit the ball. Roll the ball...and accept the outcome. Jack Burke also postulates the incontrovertible secret of putting: "Bad putting stems from thinking how instead of where."

Visualization involves the mental predisposition for anticipating a positive result. Mary Lena Faulk liked to share her putting secret with her pupils. "When it is on the putting green, the ball wants to go into the hole. It wants to disappear into the cup. Keep that in mind when you are rolling the ball into the cup. It wants to go in."

If we agree that the sole objective of putting is rolling the ball and the desired outcome is that the hole gets in the way of the rolling ball, then we are confronted with the mythology of the putter. Since the putter is the stick for rolling the ball, it is logical that the putter should be designed to enhance the desired effect. As the sweet spot on a putter expands, the rolling characteristics of the stick diminish. A common business axiom states: when everything is a priority, nothing is a priority. The putting parallel declares: when the putter face is the sweet spot, there is no sweet spot. By definition the sweet spot is the point (spot) on the putterface that is resistant to torque at impact with the ball. An expanded sweet spot is a diluted sweet spot, i.e. a semi-sweet spot. It is a compromise that produces mediocrity. A bad stroke is forgiven, but a good stroke is sacrificed in the balance.

Since putting is the most misunderstood element on the periodic chart of golf, it is naturally the most mythologized. DeBunkering the putting myths embedded in your golfing subconscious will have a profound effect on your success as a player. Rocky Thompson has a properly optimistic formula for exorcising putting demons. He carries two putters in his golf bag. He explains: "On the course I play putter gin: If the putter makes the putt, it gets to go again on the next hole. If it misses, it takes a seat in the bag until the other putter misses. I don't want any of my putters feeling too secure or they may slack off and start missing." Proactive insecurity is the essence of good putting. Roll the ball...and accept the outcome.

In *Golf Magazine*/April 1998, Tiger Woods describes an adjustment he made after his performance dropped off in the second half of 1997. He discovered that he was too worried about mechanics on the greens. The solution: "I went back to the way I used to putt as a kid. Look at it, hit it." The universal key to putting, as Mr. Nike has repeatedly emphasized in his prolific advertising campaign: "Just do it!"

Overemphasizing the importance of putting is an early warning sign for the most excruciating disease known to golfers: the dreaded yips. In a feature titled "One for the Yipper" from *Golf Magazine*/September 1982, Al Barkow identifies myriad cures for the putting impaired.

1. Close your eyes when you stroke the putt.
2. Look at the hole, not the ball.
3. Concentrate on the putter blade. Track the blade with your eyes.
4. Hole all putts, however short. Become accustomed to success.

5. Pick a spot about an inch in front of the ball and roll the ball over it.
6. Adopt a set routine (that includes a triggering movement, for example a forward press with the hands to initiate the stroke).
7. Putt cross-handed to stabilize the left wrist.
8. Avoid paralysis by remaining in motion before putting.
9. Extend the right forefinger down the grip to discourage insecurity.
10. Putt left-handed to encourage a different perspective.
11. Stroke all putts with the right hand only.
12. Select a putter with an extra thick grip to help eliminate wristiness.
13. Grip tightly: it gets blood flowing to the fingers, promotes better clubhead feel and prevents wristiness.
14. Use the "butter churn" grip.
15. Putt "Diegel-style" with elbows akimbo to lock the wrists.
16. Experiment with the "sidesaddle" method. The stroke is keyed by the left atop the grip cap acting as a hinge, while the stroke is made by the right arm.
17. See a hypnotist.
18. Place your weight on the toes of your left foot and whistle as you putt.
19. Buy an extra long putter.
20. Ingest vitamin and mineral stoked capsules containing dessicated ox bile guaranteed to cure the yips.

The putting green is the setting for two of the most derisive customs in golf: plumb bobbing and practice strokes. Plumb bobbing is an anathema that should have been outlawed with croquet-style putting. It is a prime example of over analysis that leads to confusion and paralysis. The practice stroke is an ineffective counterpart to the practice swing. They are unmistakable examples of reallocated significance i.e. unwarranted emphasis on how instead of where. Remember that the objective is reaching the target. The gauge is "How many?" Not "How?"

If all of this expert advice fails to exorcise your putting demons, ponder Leslie Nielson's cogent conundrum: "The secret of putting is not putting."

Bunker Play DeBunkered

> "There is nothing like bunkers for separating the philosophic from the unphilosophic among a golfing crowd."
>
> —unknown

Walter Hagen said: "The sand shot ought to be the easiest shot in golf. You don't even have to hit the ball." As the passing decades dim our memories of Hagen, the multitudes of golf professionals and instructors continue to echo a comparable sentiment regarding the simplicity of bunker play. My eloquently simple response to these misguided experts: "How much horse manure are you willing to accept on your ice cream cone?"

Sand save percentages are the PGA Tour's measurement of a pro's efficiency from a bunker. If we examine the facts, we will verify what the non-professional golfer already knows: "It is difficult as hell to play a sand shot."

The Facts/Sand Saves Leaders

1998 – PGA Tour
1.	Keith Fergus	71.0%
2.	Len Mattiace	69.8
3.	Kirk Triplett	66.7
4.	Fuzzy Zoeller	64.9
5.	Justin Leonard	64.4
6.	Craig Parry	63.3
7.	Stewart Cink	62.9
8.	Steve Stricker	62.9
9.	Billy Mayfair	62.7
10.	Esteban Toledo	61.5

1997 – PGA Tour
1.	Bob Estes	70.3%
2.	Ronnie Black	66.3
3.	Frank Nobilo	64.6
4.	Jay Haas	64.5
5.	Stuart Appleby	64.2
6.	John Morse	63.8
7.	Kevin Sutherland	63.8
8.	Willie Wood	62.6
9.	Lanny Wadkins	62.5
10.	Jesper Parnevik	62.4

1996 – PGA Tour
1.	Gary Rusnak	64.0%
2.	Jeff Sluman	63.4
3.	Greg Kraft	63.3
4.	Glen Day	63.2
5.	Justin Leonard	62.6

6. Wayne Grady	61.7
7. Jesper Parnevik	61.4
8. Phil Mickelson	61.3
9. Jerry Kelly	61.2
10. Brad Faxon	61.1

1998 – LPGA Tour

1. Lisa Walters	62.2%
2. Pearl Sinn	55.7
3. Val Skinner	54.3
4. Muffin Spencer-Devlin	53.3
5. Nancy Ramsbottom	52.3
6. Annette DeLuca	52.2
7. Missie McGeorge	51.9
8. Nadine Ash	51.7
9. Kathryn Marshall	51.5
10. Cindy Flom	51.2
11. Catriona Matthews	50.7
12. Wendy Ward	50.0

1998 – Senior PGA Tour

1. Jose Maria Canizares	64.4%
2. Vicente Fernandez	60.2
3. Hubert Green	58.1
4. Lee Trevino	57.6
5. Bob Duval	57.0
6. Gary Player	56.8
7. Hugh Baiocchi	56.4
8. Simon Hobday	56.1
9. Hale Irwin	56.1
10. Jim Colbert	55.6

The conclusions are obvious:

1. From 1996-1998, only two players on the PGA Tour saved par from the sand in more than seventy percent of their attempts...and they couldn't maintain that success rate longer than one year.
2. In 1998, the "best" Senior Tour players from the sand failed to save par on at least 1 of every 3 attempts. For the majority of Senior Tour players, salvaging a par from a bunker is a 50-50 proposition.
3. In 1998, only 12 players from the LPGA Tour achieved a sand save success rate greater than 50 percent.

Furthermore, skillful sand play is not a prerequisite for competitive success in golf. The 1998 sand save percentages for the top 7 players on the LPGA money list might suggest that indifferent bunker play is essential to the formula for success. The following statistics substantiate the claim. The 7 players listed below had a cumulative sand save percentage of 35.4 (167 of 472).

1998 Sand Save Statistics of Top 7 Money Winners

1.	Annika Sorenstam	32.6%	(15 of 46)
2.	Se Ri Pak	46.8	(36 of 77)
3.	Donna Andrews	29.4	(15 of 51)
4.	Karrie Webb	39.1	(27 of 69)
5.	Liselotte Neumann	35.0	(21 of 60)
6.	Juli Inkster	32.9	(25 of 76)
7.	Brandie Burton	30.8	(28 of 91)
	Total	35.4	(167 of 472)

Donald Ross said that it is the business of a player to avoid a bunker wherever it might be. I'd like to expand upon the concept of bunker avoidance by examining the top 25 money winners on the 1998 LPGA Tour and determining the average number of bunker shots each of them played per round.

	PLAYER	Rounds	Chances	Avoidance Rate
1.	Annika Sorenstam	77	46	.597
2.	Se Ri Pak	96	77	.729
3.	Donna Andrews	86	51	.593
4.	Karrie Webb	83	69	.831
5.	Liselotte Neumann	74	60	.811
6.	Juli Inkster	89	76	.854
7.	Brandie Burton	91	91	1.000
8.	Pat Hurst	93	94	1.011
9.	Meg Mallon	96	76	.792
10.	Dottie Pepper	84	66	.786
11.	Laura Davies	71	69	.972
12.	Lorie Kane	111	88	.793
13.	Danielle Ammaccapane	99	80	.808
14.	Helen Alfredson	81	58	.716
15.	Hiromi Kobayashi	88	74	.841
16.	Sherri Steinhauer	106	91	.858
17.	Kelly Robbins	80	84	1.050
18.	Rosie Jones	90	90	1.000
19.	Chris Johnson	91	102	1.121
20.	Wendy Ward	78	74	.949

21. Tammie Green	71	59	.831
22. Michelle Estill	91	87	.956
23. Emilee Klein	103	103	1.000
24. Lisa Hackney	91	82	.901
25. Lisa Walters	82	90	1.098

Sand avoidance is a calculation which measures the number of sand traps encountered per 18 holes or per round. Divide the total number of bunkers visited by the number of rounds completed. If you've found yourself in a sand trap on 10 occasions in 10 rounds of golf, then your sand trap avoidance rating (s.t.a.r.) equals 1, i.e. 10 divided by 10 equals 1. If you are only bunkered 10 times in 20 rounds of golf your s.t.a.r. is .5000, a superior performance indicative of precise shotmaking and thoughtful course management.

Who were the s.t.a.r. leaders on the LPGA Tour in 1998? I had to carry the calculation to three decimal places to determine the top s.t.a.r. among LPGA players (see below).

	PLAYER	S.T.A.R.	Money ($) Rank
1.	Donna Andrews	.593	3
2.	Annika Sorenstam	.597	1
3.	Helen Alfredson	.716	14
4.	Se Ri Pak	.729	2
5.	Dottie Pepper	.786	10

In spite of the limited evidence presented, I don't believe that I've gerrymandered the results. In fact, I think the conclusion is obvious:
Players who avoid sand traps earn large paychecks.

What is the average semiskilled hacker to do?
1. Play for the middle of the green. Bunkers are seldom located in the center of the green.
2. When you find yourself in an unavoidable bunker, don't get cute—-play for the middle of the green and just get out. Use any conceivable method of escape: explode, chip, putt.
3. Experiment with a gimmicky sand wedge. If it works, pay homage to the gods of golf technology.

Let's review.
1. The best players in the world perform miraculous escapes from the sand less than 50 percent of the time.
2. Good players consistently avoid sand traps.
3. Donald Ross was a genius.

4. Lawrence of Arabia was not a great golfer...He spent too much time in the sand.

DeBunkering Practice

> "They say 'practice makes perfect.' For the vast majority of golfers it merely consolidates imperfection."
>
> —Henry Longhurst

Conventional wisdom proclaims that golfing proficiency can only be achieved by following the proverbial prescription for getting to Carnegie Hall: "Practice! Practice! Practice!" The pre-eminent practitioner of this admonition was Ben Hogan and his contemporary disciples are legion, notably Faldo, Kite, Price, Strange, Lehman, Norman, Player and Singh to name just a few. Their dedication and exertion leads them toward the Holy Grail.

When asked to confide his "secret" for nurturing the perfect golf swing, Hogan declared: "The secret's in the dirt." The inference is that a player has to dig out a swing from hours and days and months and years of practice as Hogan had done.

Hogan's practice ethic is best expressed in the following quotes from the legendary Texan:

- "If you can't outplay them, outwork them."
- "The harder I work, the luckier I get."
- "If I miss one day's practice I know it; if I miss two days the spectators know it; and if I miss three days the world knows it." (paraphrasing Paderewski)
- "There isn't enough daylight in any one day to practice all the shots you need to practice."
- "Every day you miss practicing, it will take you one day longer to be good."

Hogan's orthodox approach to practice has become dogmatic among professionals and amateurs alike. For many of them, practice becomes a compulsive behavior. "We've done it so much for so long that it's part of our routine," acknowledges Curtis Strange. Furthermore he admits he always feels a twinge of guilt if he doesn't practice after a round. The implication is clearly overwhelming: In this formal and traditional game the remedy for all of your golfing ills is practice. You need to practice longer...you need to work harder...but it's BUNK!

Most golfers will benefit from the example of Hagen not Hogan. Walter Hagen believed it was a shame to waste great shots on the practice tee and he restricted his practice time accordingly. Obsessive practice permits no time to stop along the way to smell the flowers. Modern stars Fuzzy Zoeller and Bruce Lietzke epitomize the Haig's *laissez faire* outlook on the game. They ranked among the most successful players in the 1970s and 1980s (and they remain highly competitive today) despite minimal time on the practice range.

An anonymous genius once said: "There is nothing more wasteful than performing an unnecessary activity with great efficiency." Consider this revelation from Byron Nelson: "You can practice yourself out of a good swing as well as into one. Just hit enough balls to stay limber and in the groove." Note the distinction between practice and warming up. It is important to loosen up and stretch your muscles on the practice tee prior to a round of golf, but excessive practicing is frequently counterproductive.

Esquire, April 1998, contains this disclosure from Greg Norman to Joe Bargmann, "Now I find going to the golf course is hard work. I've done it for 21 years professionally and to stand there and hit another six hundred balls every morning, sore back, sore body, then go out and play—it doesn't have the same appeal." Is it possible that Greg would have won more than two major championship titles in 20 years if he hadn't hit 600 balls each day? How many great shots did he waste on the practice tee? Were six hundred balls each day a contributory factor to Norman's sore back and sore body?

I now call my final expert witness in our case against compulsive practicing. Bobby Jones, the dominant player of his era and arguably the greatest golfer in the history of the game, played less golf during his ascendancy than all of his contemporaries. He routinely went for months without picking up a club. In his masterpiece, *Bobby Jones on Golf*, he expounded on practice:

- "To stand upon a tee for hours banging away mechanically and monotonously at ball after ball is certainly trying on the nerves; it is also a waste of time."
- "If you cannot think of some kink to iron out or fault to correct, don't go out. And if there is a kink or a fault, as soon as it has been found and cured, stop immediately and don't take the risk of unearthing a new one or of exaggerating the cure until it becomes a blemish in itself."
- "There can be nothing more dangerous than tampering with a club that is working well, for, sooner or later, too much attention will spoil the machinery."

The conclusion is obvious. Intense practice is overrated. Heed this advice the next time your golfing skill betrays you. Select your favorite club and hit

20 or 30 balls at the range. If the results are satisfactory and your swing feels comfortable, deem your swing problem cured and take to the course with renewed confidence and a positive outlook. On the other hand, if you fall short of the desired result after hitting the designated range quota, retire from the practice tee and try again tomorrow...or next week...but always recall Harry Vardon's exhortation: "No matter what happens, keep hitting the ball."

Let's return to the differentiation between warming up and practice. Because it sets the tone for subsequent activity, the first hole is the most crucial hole in any round of golf. Practice prior to the round may lead to experimentation, and confusion and doubt. Warm up in lieu of practice. A proper warm up will help establish your rhythm, tempo and confidence. You will be ready to conquer the first hole.

And how about the practice swing? The practice swing is a rehearsal swing at an imaginary ball. The perplexed novice, after five or more respectable practice swings, addresses the ball and proceeds to dribble it 50 yards down the fairway. Afterward he inevitably laments, "If I could only hit the ball with my practice swing." If you are sufficiently warmed up, the practice swing becomes nonessential. So go ahead. Eschew a practice swing at an imaginary ball and make a solitary swing at a fixed object. There are only two probable results: your shot will be the same as always or your shot will be better. Isn't golf fun?

A discourse denouncing superfluous practice would be incomplete without assailing the most insidious form of practice: "preferred lies" or "winter rules." Nudging your ball into an artificially good lie is not golf. This abhorrent praxis is a hybrid variety of practice. "Preferred lies" undermine the spirit of the game because every round of golf becomes a practice round. The first step on the road to moderating your addiction to practice is abstinence from "winter rules."

Please be aware that practice avoidance does not demand lesson-avoidance. A timely lesson from a qualified instructor can be highly beneficial, and the learning will occur more effectively if it's achieved by playing, not practicing. In *A Woman's Guide to Better Golf*, Judy Rankin tells us how people change from the practice tee to the first tee, both mentally and emotionally. Muscles tighten and thought processes get all bound up. Six hundred balls equals the number shots (excluding putts) that a mid-handicapper would hit in twelve rounds of golf. The next time you take a lesson, skip the practice tee and nourish your instructor's fertile insight throughout twelve subsequent rounds of On-the-Job Training. There are no magic potions or miracle cures, but you can expedite your schedule for improvement by skipping the superfluous step of learning an action on the practice tee only to relearn that action as you attempt to incorporate it into a routine round of golf. The results will astound you.

Course management is the most under-utilized skill among all golfers. It is this single facet of the game that separates average players from great players. This essential tool can only be developed via OJT. Indeed, OJT is a misnomer. The key ingredient for expert course management is OJL (On-the-Job Learning). All training (instruction) is superfluous if no learning occurs. The golf course is the ideal classroom for learning the principles of course management.

Enjoyment in golf consists of playing to your expectations. To meet your usual standard consistently, you must avoid chronic and impulsive tinkering with your swing. The work ethic is not archaic but it is trumped by common sense. Common sense demands that you play the game instead of practicing. Your reward will be better performance

Busy yourself with the business of playing! **PLAY** the game!

DeBunkering Equipment

"There is a point where big is not necessarily better—only better is better."

—-Ely Callaway

"Unfortunately no golf scientist has yet invented an interlocking tongue."

—-Grantland Rice

1. **BIGGER** isn't better. It's only bigger.
2. Expensive equipment isn't better. It's only expensive.
3. Technology is overrated.

Although they are not startling observations, the foregoing statements would present an exhilarating opportunity to dispel some blatant misunderstandings about golf equipment. But why should we settle for the easy harvest from the bountiful cornucopia of equipment misconceptions? Why, indeed!

Let's begin with a list of equipment mumbo jumbo extracted from a cross section of typical advertisements for equipment. The technical phraseology is incomprehensible and meaningless.

1. Isokinetic insert technology
2. Acoustic elastomer insert for enhanced feel and sound
3. Self-squaring inset hosel for increased accuracy
4. Modified transitional perimeter weighting

5. Unique cavity design perfects the tone and feel of the club on impact.
6. Internal weighting and face progression reduce ballooning
7. Double cavity-back weighting system and power lofts for increased distance and feel
8. Invisible inset hosel allows head to rotate faster so club is square at impact
9. Boring trajectory reduces ball spin to create tumble, roll and distance
10. Thicker face along top reinforces face-crown junction for better energy transfer and feel
11. Driver features thru-bore shaft design, a thicker reinforced face and strategic internal weighting to create a hard, penetrating ball flight
12. Revolutionary scientifically optimized aerodynamic reaction dimple technologies generate more surface turbulence to reduce drag and improve aerodynamic efficiency.
13. Proprietary, ultralight shaft combines low torque for stability and low frequency for extra distance
14. Woods feature large face rotation angle for less twisting at impact and greater accuracy
15. Asymmetrical face curvature design reduces distance-robbing sidespin
16. Bulge and roll create synchronized gear effect for accuracy
17. Breakthrough technology in shaft design improves swing stability and vibration absorption for solid feel and improved shot control
18. Bigger sweet spot: ideal for players who want to hit it straight
19. Revolutionary iron pyrite-kryptonite-zirconium alloy utilized to create precision counterweights that chronosynclastically re-route clubhead to assure ideal impact

Paraphrasing Raymond Douglas Davies accurate characterization of the fashionable golfing aficionado: IN MATTERS OF GOLF CLUBS HE IS AS FICKLE AS CAN BE, 'CAUSE HE'S A DEDICATED FOLLOWER OF FASHION. Buyers beware. The sole intention of the preceding pseudo-technical descriptions is not communication but obfuscation. The consumer must not become mesmerized by mythical scientific promises. If it sounds too good to be true, it probably is.

Additional common notions about golf equipment are disturbingly troublesome, e.g. 1) the growing number of golfers who believe that the fourteen club limit is insufficient and it should be expanded because of the increasingly wide variety of implements available to the golfing public; 2) the concept that stiff-shafted clubs are essential equipment for a skillful golfer; 3) the widely accepted belief that today's "hot" golf balls are ruining the game; 4) the perpetual popularity of a totally superfluous golfing accessory, the golf glove.

The rules of golf require that a competitor may not carry more than fourteen clubs in his bag during any round of golf. This limitation has indeed become obsolete. The fourteen-club limit is an exorbitant custom. In *Fast Greens* by Turk Pipkin, Billy Hemphill's father advises: "The problem with golf is you got too many tools. You give a carpenter fourteen hammers all different weights and lengths, and I guarantee he'll come back with his thumbs beat to a bloody pulp. We don't know how hard this game is. Fact is, we're lucky to come back alive."

The fundamental issue confronting the future of the game is not the level of technology in a golfer's bag, but the amount of technology in his bag. Restricting a player to twelve clubs would simplify the game for the average golfer because he could right-size his arsenal by eliminating problematic clubs. For the advanced players, a twelve-club limit would differentiate the expert from the pretender.

Attention: USGA.

Please protect the integrity of the game.

Thank you

Strategic Misconceptions and Shotmaking Errors

> "Do or do not.
> There is no try."
> —Yoda

It is one of the most perceptive and inexplicably one of the least understood directives in the game of golf: "When it's breezy, swing easy." In essence this means that a player should always overclub when it's windy. Most of us comprehend this sage advice when we are playing into the wind. More club and an easy swing promote a lower ball trajectory with less spin. The lower trajectory allows the ball to penetrate the wind. Because a headwind accentuates our mistakes, less spin means the wind won't exaggerate an error if we mishit the shot.

Overclubbing downwind is widely misunderstood. During a friendly round at Colonial C.C. in Fort Worth, Texas, Ben Hogan advised writer Dan Jenkins that you always overclub downwind. Jenkins believed that he was the victim of a sly prank, but Hogan was dead serious. The basic greenside strategy—don't chip if you can putt; don't pitch if you can chip—is applicable to every phase of shotmaking. A player is more likely to achieve the desired result when the ball spends less time in the air. As Jim Flick has said: "Low shot = Low risk; High shot = High risk."

Even the astute and talented professional Tom Lehman is ignorant of this basic strategy. In the March/April 1998 issue of *PARTNERS*, Lehman instructs members to take a shorter club and get shots airborne when playing with the wind. This is inferior advice because allowing the wind to determine the outcome of our shot means we are at its mercy. If the wind momentarily calms or switches directions, our airborne shot is headed for disaster even if it is well struck. Windy conditions identify the shotmakers in the game. A defining characteristic of a premier shotmaker is the ability to hit the lowest shot possible under the circumstance. To summarize, the cardinal rule when it's windy: overclub and swing easy.

Bump and run is not only a strategy for combating windy conditions. Short game guru Dave Pelz exuberantly endorses the benefits of the "bump and run" over "through the air" shots. When conditions are favorable, the bump and run may be the easiest shot in golf. Simply take one more club than normal for the particular distance and make a half-swing at three-quarter speed.

There are manifold advantages to this method:

1. Because golfers tend to hit the ball more solidly on half-swings, bump and run shots consistently fly straighter.
2. Bump and run mishits lose less distance.
3. Bump and run mistakes find less trouble than miss-hit air shots.
4. Fairway contours are more forgiving of bump and run shots.
5. Wind has less effect on bump and run shots.
6. Bump and run shots generally finish in the fairway short of the green or on the green. Most air shots finish on the green or in trouble along side of the green (sand, rough or water).

It should be readily apparent why Mr. Pelz proclaimed "Bump It!" in *Golf Magazine*/November 1997.

The chip shot is the green side equivalent of the bump and run from the fairway. It is a misunderstood and under-utilized strategy. The "bank" shot, a specialized chip using a bank or hillock to the ball, is egregiously overlooked as a green side option. Select a middle iron and using your lag putting stroke, bump your chip into a bank and let it crawl up the bank to a tight pin location. As you gain confidence in this shot, it will prove more effective than a pitch or lob over an intervening bank to a tight pin. A truly exquisite shotmaker will use the same mid-iron chipping stroke to navigate a sandtrap without a lip to attack a tight pin.

It occurs at least once in every golf telecast. As veteran Quincy Quail struggles indecisively over a shot to the green, the insightful and loquacious analyst/announcer asserts: "This is a difficult yardage for Quail because he's between clubs." This comment presupposes that Mr. Quail is deficient in shotmaking ability, i.e. imagination and finesse. A shotmaker is never between clubs; he must have the skill to manufacture a shot to fit the conditions. Once again we have a skill that cannot be refined on the practice tee. Shotmaking combines a dedication to experimentation and the freedom of imagination. These are qualities that can only be nurtured in golf's ultimate classroom, the golf course.

Mental Myths

> "Ye try too hard
> and ye think too much."
> —Shivas Irons

Example 1. There are two outs in the bottom of the ninth inning and the score is tied at 2 runs apiece. It's the seventh game of the World Series. Ernie Banks, who is on second base with a double, represents the winning run for the Cubs. Dick Radatz, the Boston relief specialist, waits on the mound as Sammy Sosa steps into the batter's box. Throughout Wrigley Field dutiful ushers stand at hushed attention and woodenly raise "Quiet Please!" placards. The silence is deafening as "the Monster" begins his windup...

Example 2. It is the decisive seventh game of the NBA Finals. Wilt Chamberlain, who has come down from heaven to lead the Phoenix Suns to the Championship Finals, is fouled with 1.8 seconds remaining in the fourth quarter. The Suns are trailing the Detroit Pistons by one point and the aspirations of the entire season rest squarely on Chamberlain's shoulders as he steps to the line. Wilt has had a spectacular season, leading the league in 3-point shooting and free throw percentage (an unprecedented 98.2% from the charity stripe). The referee hands the ball to Wilt as he prepares to shoot the first of two free throws. A message on the huge electronic scoreboard overhead in the center of the arena proclaims:

"QUIET, PLEASE!!!"

Silence reigns as the ball arches toward the hoop...

Example 3. It is irrefutable that Super Bowl XLVIII will be remembered as the most competitive game in history. The scoreboard tells the tale: Venus

21, Brooklyn 21. It is fourth and ten on the fifty-yard line with 10.391 seconds remaining on the intergalactic chronometer. 750,000 fans become quiet as Venusian's quarterback Randall (don't call me Randy) Cunningham III prepares to take the crucial snap.

The examples may be puerile and mundane, but the inference is obvious: attentiveness is not contingent upon silence.

I am not advocating rebellion against the decorum of the game of golf, but the excessive admonitions for absolute silence are unwarranted. A player who is in control of his emotions and intent on the task ahead of him must certainly be oblivious to any extraneous activities surrounding him. It is the essence of concentration. It is one of the primary distinctions between the ordinary golfer and the extraordinary golfer.

DeBunkering Slow Play

> "Most golfers would play better if they thought about it less. If you are going to hit a bad shot, you ought to do it quickly. Why make a shank seem planned?"
>
> —David Owens

In *Golf Digest*/May 1986, Richard D. Haskell, former executive director of the Massachusetts Golf Association, pinpointed several factors that have contributed to the slow-play crisis pervading golf today.

1. The emphasis on winning. We no longer play golf. Now we must win at golf. Beating someone takes longer than playing with him.
2. The emphasis on scoring. Every putt must be holed for handicap purposes. There are no casual rounds. Each round is a contest.
3. Improved watering systems. Modern watering systems assure the maintenance of punishing rough that guarantees needlessly wasted time searching for lost balls.
4. More is better. There appears to be an unchecked trend toward longer courses, bigger greens, more bunkers and more water hazards. Architectural extravagance exacerbates slow play.
5. Gambling. Excessive side bets mean more bookkeeping and added pressure.
6. Faster greens. It's an inverse relationship. When the speed of the greens increases, the pace of play decreases.
7. Selfishness. More and more golfers appear to believe that "playing privileges" are a mandate to play any way they please and as slowly as they want.

8. The golf glove. In addition to being a totally superfluous accessory, the golf glove confounds golfers with the constant dilemma of deciding and re-deciding when to wear it and when not to wear it.

9. Yardage books. They were intended to be a remedy for slow play, but yardage books have slowed the pace of play as golfers march up and down the fairway measuring the distance requirement for their next shot to the nearest millimeter. This procedure becomes even more incomprehensible when we consider that most golfers seldom hit any club the same distance twice.

10. The Jack Nicklaus Syndrome. Golfers have become particularly keen at imitating Nicklaus's deliberate pace of play. The subliminal message to the golfing public is if Jack can play that way, it must be all right for me to play that way, too. If imitation is the sincerest form of flattery, Jack Nicklaus and many other professional golfers should feel immensely flattered by the pace of play at public golf courses.

Mr. Haskell's analysis is undeniably perceptive, however he fails to discern the most insipid factor in this cosmic crisis. The omnipresent motorized golf cart has perpetuated the slow play epidemic that was inspired by televised golf.

There is no more vile invention than the motorized golf cart in the entire history of mankind. The motorized golf cart is unquestionably the most decadent, destructive, aggravating and frustrating mechanism in the modern universe. A political party could assure the victory of its candidates by declaring their opposition to the perpetuation of the motorized golf cart menace.

On a less grandiose scale, golfers should boycott golf courses with motorized carts. Golfers must remain steadfast in their boycott until golf course owners comply with two non-negotiable demands: 1) deactivate every cart in their fleet; 2) remove all offensive paved cart paths. If a golf course owner is unwilling to comply with the demands of the golfing populace, he should unceremoniously rename his facility a "cartball course" and sever all ties to his golfing heritage. Golf courses would henceforth become a setting for golf. This universal exclusion must be inviolable: "NO CARTBALLERS ALLOWED!"

Irrational explanations abound among non-golfers (cartballers) concerning their perception of the causes for slow play: women; seniors; novices, etc. Cartballers perpetuate these myths to mislead real golfers in their search for a stimulating, brisk and invigorating round of golf. The cartball conspiracy has weakened the infrastructure of this magnificent game.

The time for Revolution is NOW.

Golfers of the Realm UNITE! You have nothing to lose but your cart paths.

Instructional Misconceptions

> "Every person has his own way of swinging a golf club when it comes to the tiny mannerisms, just as he has his individual way of walking and eating. He will discover the golf swing that is best suited for him and he should resist all the blandishments of lower scorers and professionals who want to make him over in their own likeness."
>
> —-Gene Sarazen

In the modern classic *The Natural Golf Swing*, George Knudson debunks popular misconceptions and misinformation about the golf swing. We are so eager to improve that we will try anything. According to Mr. Knudson, the following misconceptions can be ignored forever.

1. Grip the club firmly.
2. Keep the left arm straight.
3. When gripping the club, the V's point toward the right shoulder.
4. Sit on a seat stick.
5. At address the shaft and your left arm should form a straight line.
6. Keep your weight on the inside of your feet.
7. Keep your weight toward your heels.
8. Keep your chin up at address.
9. Set up with your right elbow lower than your left.
10. Keep your head down. (This is the number one misconception in golf. Golfers who are mesmerized by the ball feel that they have to hit it rather than swing through it).
11. Take the club back low and slow.
12. Take the club back in a straight line.
13. Bang your left heel onto the ground to start the downswing.
14. Pronate the wrists on the backswing and supinate the left wrist at impact.
15. Finish high.

Writing in *The Washington Golf Monthly*/May 1998, Wayne DeFrancesco identifies 10 stupid misconceptions that have been fueled by verbal and written instruction.

1. Try not to think.
2. Golf is 90 percent mental.
3. One magic move.

4. Just swing the clubhead.
5. The swing is one big circle.
6. Swing easy. Hit it farther.
7. Swing out to the target.
8. Hold the club like a bird.
9. Pause at the top.
10. I got it. I lost it.

Vijay Singh asserts: "I've never met a teacher who doesn't have the answer to your problems, even if it's not the right answer." Despite Mr. Singh's admonition regarding the preponderance of misleading information and blatant misconceptions, many of you will adamantly persist in pursuing formal instructional programs in your quest to improve your golfing skills. A golfer's desire for knowledge is insatiable. It behooves the inquiring golfer to determine realistic personal instructional priorities. It's your game and your swing. Don't allow a dogmatic instructor to impose his theories on your game. The following guidelines will help assure that you receive effective instructions.

How To Be A Good Pupil
1. Establish clear objectives. Essentially you should aspire to a simple effective method for playing golf. After identifying your needs, inform your instructor of your objectives. It is paramount that the student tells the instructor where they are going so when they get there they know where they're at.
2. Insist upon a dedicated instructor. If you receive instruction from more than one teacher at a time, you will compromise the method and jeopardize the results.
3. If you hit balls at a practice range, you're wasting time. Even under the watchful eye of a competent instructor, hitting balls on the practice range is an inferior simulation of "real" golf. Real golf is played on a golf course. Demand a playing lesson or no lesson at all.
4. Avoid significant swing changes. Harvey Penick said it best: "When I give you an aspirin, don't take the whole bottle." Subtle changes to your grip, stance, ball position, etc. will stimulate dramatic results.
5. Focus on results, not form. An elegant swing is not an indication of golfing prowess. The requisite skills and imagination that consistently produce the desired results can only be developed on the course. Once again a playing lesson is the appropriate format for learning.
6. Sign a contract. A competent instructor should guarantee your satisfaction or return your money. If your instructor is unwilling to enter a

money-back contract, he is probably not confident of his ability to provide adequate instruction. By not signing a contract, the instructor has substantiated the contention that most golf lessons are worthless.

When you lose your golf ball in the cow pasture of real life, you seldom find it on the first try. An instructor's job is to find one swing key that will work—-not to criticize the hundreds of faults that are hindering your game. Information overload creates paralysis and diminishes learning. But improvement can only occur through change and change demands the courage to accept the results. A good student must trust the one swing key that will unlock improvement.

Note: If you regularly play "winter rules" and routinely take "mulligans," don't waste your time on instruction since you haven't established a benchmark to measure your improvement. Finally, no matter how hard you rub, you can't polish horse manure. You may need to face the reality that golf is not your game.

Happy Golfing!

VI. Personal Lists

Can we talk? Do you relish an intimate insight into the soul of the author? Here is a totally subjective chapter. The forthcoming lists are intensely opinionated...they are mine and mine alone. Will they help you transcend the spiritual malaise in your life? Probably not. But that's okay. Social and spiritual relevance are not requisite qualities for all human activity. Without further adieu, I present my personal golf lists possessing no redeeming social, spiritual or political value. Isn't democracy grand?

My Favorite Courses That I've Never Played...and probably never will

Every golfer from the uninitiated novice to the veteran fairwayfarer has a "wish list" of courses they aspire to play. This is my list.

1. Riviera, Pacific Palisades, CA
2. Augusta National, Augusta, GA
3. The Country Club, Brookline, MA
4. Banff Springs, Banff, Alberta
5. Harbour Town, Hilton Head Island, SC
6. Southern Hills, Tulsa, OK
7. Shinnecock Hills, Southampton, NY
8. Barton Creek, Austin, TX
9. Pine Needles, Southern Pines, NC
10. Cape Breton Highlands, Ingonish, Nova Scotia

Reading List

This is my ever expanding list of titles and authors...required reading if only I can find the time...and, of course, several of them are no longer in print.

1. *Bobby Locke on Golf* – Bobby Locke (1953)

2. *Just Let Me Play* – Charlie Sifford (1992)
3. *Golfer-At-Large* - Charles Price (1982)
4. *How To Win at Weekend Golf* - Julius Boros (1964)
5. *Total Shotmaking* - Fred Couples (1995)
6. *The Education of a Woman Golfer* - Nancy Lopez (1979)
7. *My Partner, Ben Hogan* - Jimmy Demaret (1954)
8. *Pro* - Frank Beard (1970)
9. *Go For Broke* - Arnold Palmer (1973)
10. *Down the Nineteenth Fairway* - Peter Dobereiner (1983)
11. *Eighteen Holes in My Head* - Milton Gross (1959)
12. *My 55 Ways to Lower Your Golf Score* - Jack Nicklaus (1969)
13. *How to Keep Your Temper on the Golf Course* - Tommy Bolt (1969)
14. *The Truth About Golf and Other Lies* - Buddy Hackett (1968)
15. *The Walter Hagen Story* - Walter Hagen (1957)
16. *The Master of Putting* - George Low (1983)
17. *Golf: The Passion and the Challenge* - Mark Mulvoy (1977)
18. *Paul Runyan's Book for Senior Golfers* – Paul Runyan (1962)
19. *Out of the Rough: An Intimate Portrait of Laura Baugh and Her Sobering Journey* – Laura Baugh (1999)
20. *Gettin' to the Dance Floor* - Al Barkow (1986)
21. *Compact Golf* – Doug Sanders (1964)
22. *Play Championship Golf All Your Life* - Max Faulkner (1973)
23. *Graduated Swing Method* - Richard Metz (1988)
24. *Swinging Into Golf* - Ernest Jones (1946)
25. *Championship Golf* – Babe Didrikson Zaharias (1948)
26. *The World of Golf* – Peter Dobereiner (1981)
27. *101 Super Shots* – Chi Chi Rodriguez (1990)
28. *A Round of Golf with Tommy Armour* – Tommy Armour (1959)
29. *Peter Alliss' Golf Heroes* – Peter Alliss (2002)
30. *Golf's Golden Grind: The History of the Tour* – Al Barkow (1974)
31. *The Golf Swing of the Future* – Mindy Blake (1972)
32. *Unplayable Lies* – Fred Corcoran (1965)
33. *The Short Way to Lower Scoring* – Paul Runyan (1982)
34. *Master Key to Good Golf* – Leslie King (1976)
35. *The Good Sense of Golf* – Billy Casper (1980)
36. *The Glorious World of Golf* - Peter Dobereiner (1973)
37. *Mr. Dutch: The Arkansas Traveler* – Beach Leighton (1991)
38. *Come Swing With Me* – Doug Sanders (1974)
39. *Advanced Golf* – Cary Middlecoff (1957)
40. *Tommy Armour's ABC's of Golf* – Tommy Armour (1967)
41. *The Hole Truth* – Tommy Bolt (1971)
42. *The Touch System for Better Golf* – Bob Toski (1971)

43. *Tiger Woods Made Look Like a Genius* – Don Crosby (2000)
44. *Golf Has Never Failed Me* – Donald J. Ross (1996)
45. *The Heart of a Golfer* – Wally Armstrong (2002)
46. *Understanding the Golf Swing* – Manuel De La Torre (2001)
47. *I Remember Ben Hogan* – Mike Towle (2000)
48. *Blue Fairways* – Charles Stock (1999)
49. *Seasons in a Golfer's Life* – Jim Nelford (1982)
50. *Old Man: The Biography of Walter J. Travis* – Bob Labbance (2002)
51. *Links* – Lorne Rubenstein (1991)
52. *Touring Prose: Writings on Golf* – Lorne Rubenstein (1992)
53. *The Brainy Way to Better Golf* – Doug Ford (1961)
54. *1001 Reasons to Love Golf* –Mar Hubert/Tiegreen Pedroli (2003)

ATTENTION: Family, friends and relatives. Any title from this list makes an ideal gift. It doesn't matter whether it's for my birthday, Christmas or some other special occasion.

—The MANAGEMENT

Practice Drills

Drills serve two purposes: simple effective warm up and routine swing maintenance. These are my favorite drills for warming up prior to a round and for maintaining a supple swing motion without spending hours on the practice tee.

WARM UP DRILLS (Before you tee off)
1. Stretch the large muscles. Work the kinks out.
2. The baseball swing: stride and swing a club like a baseball bat.
3. Perform ten to twenty left-handed golf swings.

MAINTENANCE DRILLS (At home or in the office)
1. The palm-to-palm drill: Clasp your palms and repeat your full swing motion.
2. Swing a broom or weighted club.
3. Attend a PGA or LPGA tournament and direct a critical eye at the technique of your favorite pros. Empower yourself to incorporate all applicable facets of the pro swing. The eminent golf authority Yogi Berra once said: "You can observe a lot by watching."
4. Squeeze a tennis ball.
5. Develop an isometric routine.

Hole(s)-In-One
1. Exeter GC - May 20, 1975
2.
3.

Negative Numbers on the Charisma Scale
If I were to rank golfers on a scale of 1 to 10 based on charisma, the golfers listed below would receive negative numbers. This ranking is not a reflection of talent, ability or individual accomplishments. It does reflect an excessive lack of personality and golfing appeal for the rankees (them) by the ranker (me). My list doesn't generate the notoriety as an auspicious fashion list by Mr. Blackwell, but some day it may. Without further adieu, allow me to divulge my list of golfers that only a mother could love.

1. Tom Kite
2. Steve Elkington
3. Mark Brooks
4. Jeff Maggert
5. Colin Montgomerie
6. Scott Hoch
7. Jesper Parnevik
8. Scott Verplank
9. Bob Estes
10. Tom Kite*

*Mr. Kite is phlegmatic enough to occupy two spots on this list.

It is noteworthy that no senior golfers appear on this list. There is a rejuvenation process that occurs when a golfer reaches fifty and joins the Senior PGA Tour. This rejuvenation process transforms unexciting personalities and previously invisible performers such as Miller Barber and Orville Moody become appealing senior players. Unfortunately, Tom Kite is the exception that proves the rule. Even as a senior golfer he continues to generate negative numbers on the charisma scale.

Slump Busting
This is my list of uncommon adjustments for breaking out of a slump. I use them. They work for me. I'm feeling pressure to perform well. The harder I try, the worse I play. These simple tricks help remind me that it's only a game. By placing less pressure upon myself, I relax and my "good" scores return.

1. Play for Bogey.
   I've begun my round with a few "dreaded others." Instead of attempting risky shots, I reset my priorities and play for bogey.
2. Remove Clubs from your bag.
   Too many clubs…too many decisions.
3. Change Clubs.
4. Change Balls.
5. Play without a Glove.
6. Wear your Rally Cap.
7. Play from a Different set of Tee Markers.
8. Change Partners.
9. CHANGE SOMETHING!

The Masters of Women's Golf

Dick Aultman and Ken Bowden wrote the definitive instruction manual in 1975, *The Methods of Golf's Masters*. Personally, I'm awaiting the distaff sequel. I believe that the following female should occupy the pages of this magnum opus.

1. Glenna Collett Vare
2. Joyce Wethered
3. Babe Didrikson Zaharias
4. Patty Berg
5. Louise Suggs
6. Betsy Rawls
7. Mickey Wright
8. Kathy Whitworth
9. Sandra Haynie
10. Joanne Gunderson Carner
11. Judy Rankin
12. Donna Caponi
13. Pat Bradley
14. Nancy Lopez
15. Betsy King

Happy Golfing!

VII. Incomplete Lists

This is the reader participation chapter of the book. I've exercised my pre-rogative as the author to originate unfinished lists in several provocative cat-egories. This is your opportunity to be proactive. Your assignment, if you decide to accept it, is to complete each list in an expert and scholarly man-ner. It's your chance to provide responses instead of sitting casually on the sideline. Go ahead and reach for the gusto!

The first list is a collection of quotations—some are memorable and insightful; others are humorous and outrageous. You should finish off 34 through 45 by listing suitably appropriate quotations. If you accumulate more than the requisite 14 quotes, feel free to take a blank piece of paper and continue your list by starting with 41.

Last of all, if you are a novice listmaker, let me offer this standard for-mat which can be utilized for any generic list:

(Title)

1.

2.

3.

4.

5.

6.

7.

8.

9.

10.

Directions:
1) place the name of your list in the location marked "Title"
2) fill the numbered blanks with information appropriate to the "Title"
3) add further numbers if your list exceeds 10 items, e.g. 11, 12, 13, etc.

It's that simple. With very little training you can become a professional listmaker, too.

Quotable Quotes

If Yogi Berra had been a professional golfer: "Good putting will beat good driving and vice versa."

1. "I don't know why we curse and pray to the gods of golf. Do they live only in our minds, or are we, the mortal golfers, the product of their invention? No one really knows, of course, because it's a question meant for keener minds than those who take up sticks and balls as an unwitting form of worship." —Turk Pipkin
2. "Watching Sam Snead practice hitting golf balls is like watching a fish practice swimming." —John Schlee
3. "Not much about golf really turns your stomach, does it? Why, the sport doesn't even have owners! There's a thought to make you smile all day––a game without owners."—Thomas Boswell
4. "Tommy Bolt's putter has spent more time in the air than Lindbergh."—Jimmy Demaret
5. "I've thrown or broken a few clubs in my day. In fact, I guess at one time or another I probably held distance records for every club in the bag."—Tommy Bolt
6. "He told me just to keep the ball low."—Chi Chi Rodriguez, putting advice from his caddy
7. "Putting is driving me out of the game. It's just become too painful. You

do everything perfectly, and the ball still won't go into the hole. When I putt, my emotions collide like tectonic plates. It's left my memory circuits full of scars that won't heal."—Mac O'Grady

8. "Golf is meant to be playable and enjoyable, not solvable."—Michael Cawley

9. "Golf is a cruel game, Charlie Brown."—Linus

10. "For golfers, our brains seem to shrink as we near the course. I've often thought that Lucy from 'Peanuts' could get rich if she'd place her psychiatrist booth twenty yards from the first tee."—Judy Rankin

11. "Concentration is thinking of a few things; confusion is thinking of a lot of things."—Chuck Cook

12. "I play the game because my sole ambition is to do well enough to give it up."—David Feherty

13. "Golf and masturbation have at least one thing in common: both are a lot more satisfying to do than they are to watch."—Anonymous

14. "Golf is the most overtaught and least learned endeavor. If they taught sex the way they teach golf, the race would have died out years ago."—Jim Murray

15. "There are three types of bad shots in golf: those that cost you a half stroke, those that cost you a full stroke and those that cost you two strokes. Only stupidity costs you more than two strokes."—Bob Toski

16. "Not a week goes by without my learning something new about golf. That means, of course, that I was ignorant of eight things about golf two months ago. Extend that process back nearly twenty years and the result is an impressive accumulation of ignorance."—Peter Dobereiner

17. "The only thing good about the old days is talking about them."—Bill Mehlhorn

18. "You can't let anyone, especially someone you don't know, tell you how to play a shot. If you do, then you're not playing your game. And if you're not playing your game, you might as well not play at all."—Harry Brady

19. "Some of the best lessons I've had in my life came while I was lying in bed at night just thinking about my game."—Byron Nelson

20. "There's an old saying on tour: 'Set fire to the tees and cover the greens with broken glass; put the pros out there in gasoline-soaked pants and barefooted...and someone will break par.'"—Tommy Bolt

21. "Everyone needs second chances...I sometimes think that's why we like golf so much—every round is like a second chance to finally get it right."—Opti the Mystic

22. "The guy who believes in happy endings is going to play consistently better golf than the man who approaches every act of existence with fear and foreboding."—Tony Lema

23. "Sunday golf is something religiously avoided (since my I've teenage

years, mostly) because I'm philosophically averse to any round that takes longer than childbirth."—William Hallberg

24. "It takes more than sinew; Comes down to what's in you."—Philoctetes

25. "Golf is a puzzle without an answer. You end up knowing a lot about nothing. I've won so many different ways, with so many different theories and thoughts. Nothing works for very long. It's a constant search. I've learned there are no absolutes in golf. You name me a player who does it one way, I'll name you one just as successful who does the opposite."—Gary Player

26. "Golf is a day spent in a round of strenuous idleness."—William Wordsworth

27. "Having fun while playing poorly is a skill that the instruction books rarely touch on and not every golfer can master. My problem is one that I'll bet more than a few other hackers out there suffer from: There's so much pleasure to be had playing bad golf that I don't know that I'll ever summon up the motivation to get better."—David Sands

28. "If you want to hit the ball farther, don't hit it harder, hit it better." — George Bayer

29. "Albert Einstein's theory of relativity says that the closer a person comes to moving at the speed of light, the slower time travels. Therefore, the faster you play golf, the longer it will take for you to get older."—Gary McCord

30. "Yes, I'll marry you, but first you've got to lose the lime green, checkered golf pants that look like a table cloth from an Italian restaurant."—Susy Miller/March 1990

31. "You're lucky because your right leg is shorter than your left, so you're always playing off an uphill lie—unless, of course, you're downhill and then it's level."—John Elliott

32. "Physical effort seldom solves mental problems. When a golfer misses a tee shot because too much tension affected his posture, rhythm, swing plane, or other fundamentals, he's more likely to try to make a physical correction than use his mental skills to lower his tension. Instead of solving the *real* problem, he spends the entire round working on his swing and getting more tense, instead of relaxing and giving his trained and natural swing a real chance to execute. By the end of the round, he'll be exhausted, confused, and worst of all, feel little or no confidence in what were probably sound fundamentals to begin with."—Dr. Deborah Graham

33. "You have to love every hole just like all the other holes, or the other holes will get jealous."—Alison Hurt

34.

35.

36.

37.

38.

39.

40.

41.

42.

43.

44.

45.

(Find a blank piece of paper and continue your list).

Hybrid Golfers
1. Johnny Miller Barber
2. David Graham Marsh
3. Bob Charles Coody
4. Justin Leonard Thompson
5. Jerry Kelly Gibson
6. Payne Stewart Cink

7.

8.

9.

10.

11.

12.

13.

14.

15.

I'm still searching for the elusive triple hybrid.

Best Scramblers

> "True scramblers are thick-skinned. And they always beat the whiners."
>
> —Paul Runyan

1. Walter Hagen
2. Seve Ballesteros
3. Tom Watson
4. Arnold Palmer
5. Kathy Whitworth
6. Paul Runyan
7.
8.
9.
10.
11.
12.

Caution: Your responses may incite debate, controversy or outright altercation.

50 Ways That a Golf Ball Can Enter the Hole

Paul Simon suggested that "there must 50 ways to leave your lover." In *Mulligan's Name Was Ambrose*, Tod McGinley asks us to count the ways that a golf ball can enter the hole. McGinley is the source for numbers 1 through 11. Your inimitable author added numbers 12 through 17. The rest is up to you and your powers of observation.

1. The ball can topple into the hole like a "dying" putt by Jack Nicklaus.
2. The ball can bang the back of the hole like a "charging" putt by Arnold Palmer.
3. The ball can plunge into the hole like a skydiver whose chute is reluctant to unfurl.
4. The ball can crawl into the hole like your neighbor coming home at 3 A.M.
5. The ball can swagger into the hole like John Wayne entering the swinging doors of Rose's Cantina.
6. The ball can skip into the hole like Richard Simmons leading an exercise group.
7. The ball can plummet into the hole like the FAA's description of a plane crash as "a controlled flight into terrain."
8. The ball can plop into the hole like a cow splattering the floor of the barn.
9. The ball can stumble into the hole like Red Skelton doing a skit in an antique shoppe.
10. The ball can tumble into the hole like a scuba diver going overboard backward into the sea.
11. The ball can slam into the hole like Michael Jordan dunking a basketball from high above the rim.
12. The ball can bump into the hole like a blind squirrel finding an acorn.
13. The ball can circle the hole like a weary world traveler.
14. The ball can slink into the hole like a cautious thief.
15. The ball can enter the hole like a servant through the service entrance.
16. The ball can sneak into the hole like a reluctant guest.
17. The ball can be trapped against the pin like a crayfish beneath a rock.

18.

19.

20.

21.

22.

23.

24.

25.

26.

27.

28.

29.

30.

31.

32.

33.

34.

35.

36.

37.

38.

39.

40.

41.

42.

43.

44.

45.

46.

47.

48.

49.

50.

III's
1. Notah Begay III
2. Davis Love III
3. Tommy Armour III
4. P. H. Horgan III
5. William A. Hyndman III
6. Harry Hurt III

7.

8.

9.

10.

If Absorbine Jr. had a son, would he be called Absorbine III?

Luck Loading
1. intentionally run over a pothole
1. befriend a black cat
3. step on a crack in the sidewalk
4. walk under a ladder
5. deliberately scratch during a pool game
6. make a list of **13** items
7. volunteer for jury duty

8.

9.

10.

11.

12.

13.

14.

15.

In *The Gods of Golf*, Smith and Holms describe "luck loading" as the pre-meditated performance of unlucky activities prior to a round of golf. Since Nature seeks balance, she will compensate your run of bad luck with a run of good luck on the golf course. Please add specific unlucky activities to the preceding list and plan to perform a minimum of three unlucky activities immediately prior to your next round of golf. Your luck will abound. Caution: 1) DO NOT share your luck loading formula with other members of your regular foursome. Since the overall supply of luck is limited, there may not be enough to go around. 2) Ostracize beginners from your foursome. Neophyte's serendipity will negate any attempt at luck loading.

Greatest Putters
Crenshaw: "…players don't like great putters. They know that putting gets these players over the hump sometimes, and they scoff at that. They admire ball striking but not putting."

1. Billy Casper
2. Bobby Locke
3. Ben Crenshaw
4. Bob Charles
5. Brad Faxon
6. Horton Smith
7. Walter J. Travis
8. Loren Roberts
9.
10.
11.
12.

Grantland Rice: "Walter J. Travis could do more with a putter than any golfer in history…(H)e could…use the putter effectively off the green and from bunkers where the ball was lying well."

Corey Pavin: "Putting is shotmaking, too."

Alliterative Golfers/Past and Present

AA   Amy Alcott
BB   Brad Bryant
CC   Charles Coody
DD   David Duval
EE   Ernie Els
FF   Fred Funk
GG   Gibby Gilbert
HH   Harold Hilton
II
JJ
KK
LL
MM
NN
OO
PP
QQ
RR
SS
TT
UU
VV
WW
XX
YY
ZZ

I've done the easy part. The challenge is to find 26 alliterative golfers: one for each letter of the alphabet. Hint: Ziggy Zoeller, Zorro Zarley, Zeke Zokol and Zsa Zsa Zaharias are not correct responses, however Sam Snead, Sandra Spuzich and Steve Stricker are correct.

Quirky Swings

1. Gay Brewer
2. Miller Barber
3. Jim Furyk
4. Ray Floyd
5. Lee Trevino
6. Doug Sanders
7. Moe Norman
8. Jacky Cupit

9.

10.

11.

12.

There are probably several members of your regular foursome who belong on this list. My wife insists that I could be a charter member of The Quirky Swing Club.

The Animal Channel

1. Red Hawk GC, Temecula, CA
2. Eagle Nest GC, North Myrtle Beach, SC
3. Buffalo Hill GC, Kalispell, MT
4. Whitefish GC, Pequot Lakes, MN
5. Shark River GC, Neptune, NJ
6. Wolf Run GC, Zionsville, IN
7. Buck Hill GC, Buck Hill Falls, PA
8. Raccoon Hill GC, Kent, OH
9. Quail Hollow GC, Boise, ID
10. Beaver Meadow GC, Concord, NH
11. Otter Creek GC, Ankeny, IA
12. Moose Run GC, Fort Richardson, AK
13. Fox Squirrel CC, Southport, NC

14.

15.

16.

17.

18.

19.

20.

Nicknames
1. The Squire
2. The Haig
3. Champagne Tony
4. Gene the Machine
5. The Walrus
6. The Arkansas Traveler
7. The Silver Scot

8.

9.

10.

11.

12.

No further information is necessary; the player and the nickname are synonymous.

Superlative Shots
1. Gene Sarazen, 15th hole at Augusta National GC, final round of The Masters, 1935.
2. Bobby Jones, 17th hole at Royal Lytham & St. Anne's, final round of the British Open, 1926.
3. Larry Mize, 11th hole at Augusta National GC, second playoff hole of The Masters, 1987.
4. Arnold Palmer, 15th hole at Royal Birkdale, final round of the British

Open, 1961.
5. Tom Watson, 17th hole at Pebble Beach, final round of the US Open, 1982.
6. Bob Tway, 18th hole at Inverness, final round of the PGA Championship, 1986.
7. Hale Irwin, 18th hole at Medinah, final round of the US Open, 1990.

8.

9.

10.

11.

12.

13.

14.

Final round and playoff heroics in a major championship are key—if not essential—criteria for determining my contributions to the superlative shot list. Your criteria may vary to include a random act of chance that occurred while playing with your regular foursome. Consider this extraordinary achievement by Zeppo Marx: "The hardest shot is the mashie at ninety yards from the green, where the ball has to be played against an oak tree, bounces back into a sandtrap, hits a stone, bounces on the green and then rolls into the cup. That shot is so difficult I have only made it once." This is truly an example of superlative shotmaking and it may be worthy of inclusion on *your* list.

Arbor Day
1. Pine Valley CC, Wilmington, NC
2. Oak Hill CC, Milford, NJ
3. Cottonwood Valley CC, Irving, TX
4. Dogwood Hills GC, Chillocothe, OH
5. Apple Tree GC, Yakima, WA
6. Cypress Bay GC, Little River, SC
7. Lone Palm GC, Lakeland, FL
8. Hickory Hill GC, Methuen, MA

9. Maple Dale CC, Dover, DE
10. Birch Creek GC, Smithfield, UT
11. Peachtree GC, Atlanta, GA

12.

13.

14.

15.

16.

17.

18.

19.

20.

Classic Examples of Supination

Manipulation of the clubhead with the hands so that the clubhead is ahead of the hands at impact is known as pronation. It is exactly opposite of what the player wants. At impact the back of the left hand should point at the target. The wristbone is raised and the wrist is nearer the target than any other part of the hand. This is known as supination. Ben Hogan identified supination of the left wrist as an essential characteristic for great ball-striking.

1. Ben Hogan
2. Byron Nelson
3. Tom Weiskopf
4. Ken Venturi
5. Gardner Dickinson

6.

7.

8.

9.

10.

Spellchecker
1. Lanny Wadkins = Lanai Wackiness
2. Jesper Parnevik = Jester Parvenu
3. Annika Sorenstam =Unique Sorrento
4. Seve Ballesteros = Seven Balusters
5. Liselotte Neumann = Isolate Neuron
6. Vic Ghezzi = Vice Ghetto
7. Deane Beman = Deafen Bemoan
8. Missie McGeorge = Missile Max McGregor
9. Brent Geiberger = Brunt Gembrewer

10.

11.

12.

13.

14.

Golf at the Cinema
1. A Gentlemen's Game (2002)
2. The Caddy (1953)
3. Caddyshack (1980)
4. Tin Cup (1996)
5. Goldfinger (1964)
6. Banning (1967)
7. Follow the Sun (1951)
8. The Legend of Baggar Vance (2000)
9. M*A*S*H (1970)

10.

11.

12.

13.

14.

Golf has an unrivalled literary tradition, but cinematically golf scores a double bogey: two thumbs down!

Golfing Equations
1. Feel = Imagination
2. Analysis = Paralysis
3. Simplicity = Solution
4. Low Shot = Low Risk

5.

6.

7.

8.

9.

10.

11.

12. *Donald's Book of Golf Lists* = Brilliant Masterpiece

More Basic Swing Types
…Continued

1. Pick and Peck
2. The Chicken Wing
3. Fire and Fall Back
4. The Corkscrew
5. Wiggle, Waggle and Whiff
6. The Agrarian

7. Slash and Dash
8. The Ferris Wheel
9. The Bossa Nova
10. Foot Wedge and Hand Mashie

11.

12.

Upon completing this list you will possess an embryonic outline for an erudite doctoral thesis. Categorization, classification and examination of the infinite varieties of golf swings will unlock the secrets of the metaphysical universe.

The Very Best Golfing Destinations on the Planet

1. Ireland
2. Scotland
3. Bermuda
4. Hawaii
5. San Diego
6. Nova Scotia
7. Jekyll Island, GA
8. Brooksville, FL

9.

10.

11.

The initial entries on this list are some of the typical responses for the destination of an ideal golf vacation. They reflect varying combinations of affluence, tradition, prestige and allure. As you can see, the criteria for the "best" vacation destinations are very subjective. It is very possible that your idea of a great golfing vacation includes a six pack and an excursion to Hooters.

Happy Golfing!

VIII. The Final Elbow

The following is a completely unbiased and unsolicited testimonial. After rereading and carefully reviewing the contents of *Hole-In–One Pair of Pants*, I can only draw one conclusion: If I discovered this book on the shelf of my favorite bookstore, I would buy it...or at least add it to my "reading list" and suggest that a generous family member or friend make me the exuberant recipient of what is sure to be a cherished gift.

It's now time for some profound and quintessential lists. I've saved the best for last. Trust me. Would I lie to you?

Ultimate Reality

> "Your best golf is something you never own. It's
> just something you've borrowed for a while."
> —-Dave Marr

Your next round could be the best you ever played...or the worst you ever played. What is the ultimate reality?

1. Just accept it and save your friends, family and relatives the tedious dissertations on how great or how lousy you are.
2. A healthy attitude toward the game focuses on the journey, not the destination.
3. When the game is exhilarating, act humble. The golf gods don't take kindly to gloating.
4. When you're not up to form, hang in there. Avoid whining and do whatever it takes to get yourself back to where you want to be.
5. The better you get, the better the chance that tomorrow will be as good as today is.
6. The journey to golfing mastery is about segregating proper ideas from

misconceptions and learning to execute those ideas on the golf course.

7. Golf is an objective game. The ball and the club don't care about the shot you're facing. It's up to you to execute the shots at your favorite local golf course.

—-from *The Washington Golf Monthly*/May 1998: "10 Stupid Things..." by Wayne DeFrancesco

Top 40

Caution: If any of the subsequent tips fail to transform your game, immediately assign them to the Misconception File.

1. Good driving is the foundation of a good game.
2. The average player tees the ball too low for the drive.
3. Fingers secure, arms relaxed.
4. In gripping the club, you should feel pressure in the hands but not in the forearms.
5. Walk with a steady, relaxed rhythm while swinging your arms freely.
6. Posture gives your arms room to swing.
7. Don't overswing on the backswing.
8. Low Shot = Low Risk; High Shot = High Risk
9. Always overclub downwind.
10. Use a more lofted club from a bad lie.
11. Use flexible shafts and soft grips.
12. Leave the flagstick in when chipping.
13. Creating the proper trajectory makes more sense than trying to create spin.
14. Use a putter instead of chipping whenever possible.
15. Regardless of where a bunker might be, it is the business of the player to avoid it.
16. The ball goes where the sand goes.
17. The majority of short putts are missed by looking for imaginary slopes.
18. If a hole doesn't fit your eye, create a shot with a club you wouldn't ordinarily use.
19. When in dire straits, you can always use the stroke-and-distance penalty option.
20. Catch yourself doing something right.
21. Don't be so scientific as to lose all dash.
22. The most successful way to play golf is the easiest way.
23. The best time orientation you can have on the golf course is the precious present. Just hit it!
24. The best way to play golf is the simplest.

25. If you're not playing your game, you might as well not play at all.
26. The best way to swing is the simplest way.
27. Never fight your eye when you look at the hole.
28. If a hole doesn't fit your eye, create something.
29. Expect the ball to follow your mental plan for it.
30. Know your clubs.
31. Putting is shotmaking.
32. If you want to hit the ball farther, hit it better.
33. The swing that you take at a cigar stump is usually the right one.
34. You can't play golf with a frightened heart.
35. Never aim for a hazard.
36. Golfers who swing too fast have a tough time coordinating their arms and legs.
37. If you're not sure about the break, just hit it at the hole.
38. Physical effort seldom solves mental problems.
39. Physical effort seldom solves mental problems.
40. Don't ever think that you understand the golf swing.

Some of the "Chosen Truths" of the Swedish National Golf Team

"On the golf course I'm only interested in golf scores, not golf swings."

—Pia Nilsson

1. Human beings are always more important than their performances.
2. Human beings have unlimited potential.
3. Each human being is unique.
4. Mind and body are one system.
5. Golf is fun.
6. It is possible to play 18 holes in 54 strokes.
7. Swedish golfers are good putters.

—from "Stalking the Perfect Round' by Lorin Anderson, *Golf Magazine*/November 1997

What You Need to Shoot a 54

1. You need a swing that suits you.
2. You need to practice in a way that suits you and results in achieving your goals.
3. You need clubs that match you, your swing and your play.
4. You need to play a ball that suits you and your game.
5. You need to play practice rounds in such a way that you learn what you

need to learn about the course.

6. You need a healthy physique that allows you to play the golf that you want.
7. You need a healthy diet that gives the nutrition you need to perform your best.
8. You need rest for your mind and your body to perform at their best.
9. You need to be able to listen to signals within you, and if something doesn't feel right, know what you can do to regain your balance so that the necessary conditions exist for playing your best golf.
10. You need to be motivated in what you do.
11. You need to believe in what you're doing.
12. You need to have clear objectives.

—-from *Different Strokes* by Mona Vold

The "need" list doesn't vary with your target. Even if your target isn't 54, the preceding list is a sound formula for achieving your potential.

Famous Last Words

Every golfer yearns to finish the round with a flourish: a birdie on the 18th hole; a forty footer for par; any memorable shot to "bring me back again." Your beloved author/listmaker attempts to exit with grace and style by disclosing 20 penultimate quotes from famous golfers and pseudo celebrities…some are real…and some are fictional…and some are anonymous.

> "I wonder if I did the right thing when I quit school and went into golf. Maybe I should have kept going and gone to Yale like my brother who's a teacher…I wonder until I look out the window and see that golf course. Then I realize how much enjoyment I've gotten out of the game, and I don't wonder any more."
>
> —John Shippen

1. "Hello, I must be golfing." —Golfo Marx
2. "That's why I keep playing golf. A voice inside my head tells me I'm still improving." —Corey Pavin
3. "What bunker?" —Lawrence of Arabia
4. "…if God intended me to play golf He would have made me (a) blonder; (b) lankier; and (c) more inclined to embrace Jesus." —Lee Eisenberg
5. "Golfingly yours, The Haig." —Walter Hagen
6. "The best part of golf is that if you observe the etiquette, you can always

find a game. I don't care how good you play, you can find somebody who can beat you, and I don't care how bad you play, you can find somebody you can beat." —Harvey Penick

7. "Remember, not even the best players in the world hit all the greens in regulation." —Tom Watson
8. "Let's tee that sucker up, and plaaaaaaaaay golf!" —Leslie Nielsen
9. "I golf, therefore I am." —Lighthorse Rene Descartes
10. "Good putting trumps good driving…and vice versa." —Yogi Birdie
11. "Let us just say that we should be grateful for the contributions all have made and realize that even though the top players have reaped rich rewards from their skill, they have also provided for the game an immense stimulus that has made it a much more enjoyable and attractive pastime for the average golfer, who, after all, is the guy—-or bloke, or whatever you choose to call him—-who supports the game." —Bobby Jones
12. "It's impossible to teach you to play as well as you hope you'll play because you'll never work on your golf as hard as you hope at it." —Tommy Armour
13. "They say golf is like life, but don't believe them. Golf is more complicated than that." —Gardner Dickinson
14. "It's a beautiful day. Let's play 36!" —Ernie 'Mr. Club' Shanks
15. "You're away." (only words) —Ben Hogan
16. "I never met a club I wouldn't throw." —Will Rogers Bolt
17. "I'll be back!" —Arnold Schwarzengolfer
18. "For purposes of clarity and simplicity, a fifteen foot putt will be considered to be five feet longer than a ten foot putt. The only notable exception to this postulation occurs when the player neglects to utilize his dominant eye while plumb bobbing a putt. This egregious violation of natural law and decorum generally results in chronosynclastic instability accompanied by an overwhelming delusion that putting is purely mental. The inherent conclusion is foregone: psychic transmogrification defies political reality. QED" —Anonymous
19. "More! More! More! Give me more! *Hole-In-One Pair of Pants* is the greatest (only) book of its kind. It's the sort of thing Shakespeare would have written if he had written this sort of thing. I can hardly wait for the sequel: *Hole-In-One Pair of Socks, Darn It.*" —John Q. Publinks

Tale of the Tiger

"No book about golf in the modern era should conclude with anyone other than Tiger Woods."

—Donald Miller

1. Born: December 30, 1975 in Cypress, California
2. U.S. Junior Amateur Champion: 1991; 1992; 1993
3. U.S. Amateur Champion: 1994; 1995; 1996
4. In 1996, Tiger joins Jack Nicklaus (1961) and Phil Mickelson (1990) as the only players to win the NCAA Championship and the U.S. Amateur in the same year.
5. August 29—September 1, 1996: In his first tournament as a professional, Tiger shoots 67-69-73-68-277 (T60) in the Greater Milwaukee Open and earns $2544.
6. PGA Tour Rookie of the Year in 1996
7. In 1997, Tiger Woods wins The Masters with a record score of 270 (18 under par). Tiger wins by a record margin of 12 strokes, a comparable margin to Young Tom Morris's 12-stroke victory in the 1870 British Open. The 12-stroke margin of victory in a major championship is exceeded only by Old Tom Morris's 13-stroke margin in the 1862 British Open.
8. August 15, 1999: Tiger wins the PGA Championship at Medinah C.C. in a memorable showdown with Sergio Garcia.
9. "My father has always instilled in me there are only two things in life that you ought to do. You gotta care and you gotta share."—Tiger Woods
10. January 1, 2000-December 31, 2000: "The Year of the Tiger." The Year 2000 joins 1913, 1930, 1945, 1953 and 1960 as the most significant years in the history of golf.

Happy Golfing!

Afterword I

by Susy Miller

I'm the wife. I met the author for the first time while traveling with a group of friends in a rented van to the 1987 Women's U. S. Open at the Plainfield Country Club in Edison, NJ. You have to know, up front, that I thought Donald Miller was the weirdest guy I had ever met. He spent the entire day walking the golf course, spouting esoteric factoids and mundane statistics that I couldn't imagine anyone in their right mind would be interested in. It got so bad that I actually made it my mission that day to bust his inane chops as often as possible. He was a sitting duck at a cheap carnival booth and I was taking pot shots at him all day long. At one point, I actually ripped the jaunty golf cap off his head and chucked it just to get him to shut up. And all he did was look at me and laugh…and then he kept right on yapping. Where in the world did this guy COME from?

Believe it or not, 3 years later I married him at Twin Lakes Country Club in Allentown, PA, in the clubhouse overlooking the 18th hole. Go figure. If you had told me that day in July 1987, that I was destined to wed Donald Miller, I'd have asked you what the hell were you smoking?

Funny thing is, the man's love for all things golf has been a driving force in his life since the age of 12, when he taught himself how to swing using an inverted cane while smacking whiffle baseballs across a farm field. From there he graduated to cheap used clubs, hitting old golf balls at the barn, which punched holes in the roof. He slept, got up, ate, worked, golfed, ate and slept again, day in and day out, all the while absorbing everything he could wrap his brain around that had anything to do with golf. I don't know about you, but in my book, that's called passion. And THAT'S why I married the weirdest guy I ever met. I'm a sucker for passion.

Afterword II

by Ronald Marple

"I may not be very sophisticated, but I'm smart enough to know when someone is peeing on my boots and calling it a rainstorm!"

—-the Sheriff in
"The Best Little Whorehouse in Texas"

If you're reading this, obviously you didn't heed my advice in the Foreword of this book. It must have been humiliating to be duped by Mr. Miller's eclectic literary musings. I'm going to offer you a second chance to follow my wise counsel. Please do all of the following:

1. Visit a hypnotist. Ask him to cleanse your minds of all sinister golf blasphemies contained in this abhorrent volume.
2. Burn your copy of *Donald's Book of Golf Lists* and scatter the ashes about the parking lot of Barnes & Noble.
3. Establish a picket line outside of Mr. Miller's residence. Maintain a 24/7 vigil until he provides a sworn affidavit stating he will never write another book.
4. Order Chinese Food for an indigent werewolf.

Bibliography

1. Alexander, et al, *The Hogan Mystique* (1994)
2. Armour, *How to Play Your Best Golf All the Time* (1953)
3. Barkow, *The History of the PGA Tour* (1989)
4. Barry, *Dave Barry Turns 40* (1990)
5. Barton & Yun, *Golf on the Web* (1997)
6. Blanchard, *Playing the Great Game of Golf* (1992)
7. Boomer, *On Learning Golf* (1942)
8. Chieger and Sullivan, *Inside Golf* (1985)
9. Coop, *Mind Over Golf* (1993)
10. Cornish and Whitten, *The Golf Course* (1981)
11. Couples, *Total Shotmaking* (1995)
12. Doak, *The Anatomy of a Golf Course* (1992)
13. Feinstein, *A Good Walk Spoiled* (1995)
14. Flick, *On Golf* (1997)
15. Floyd, *The Elements of Scoring* (1998)
16. Gallwey, *The Inner Game of Golf* (1979)
17. Graham and Stabler, *The 8 Traits of Champion Golfers* (1999)
18. Hallberg, *The Soul of Golf* (1997)
19. Hogan, *The Modern Fundamentals of Golf* (1957)
20. Hogan, *Power Golf* (1948)
21. Hurt III, *Chasing the Dream* (1997)
22. Hutchinson, *Hints On Golf* (1886)
23. Jones, *Bobby Jones On Golf* (1966)
24. Jones and Keeler, *Down the Fairway* (1927)
25. Kaydos, *Measuring, Managing, and Maximizing Performance* (1991)
26. Knudson, *The Natural Golf Swing* (1988)
27. Kreismer, *Stocking Stumpers: Golf* (1999)
28. Lema, *Golfer's Gold* (1964)
29. McAllister, *The Green* (1999)

30. McGinley, *Mulligan's Name Was Ambrose* (1998)
31. Middlecoff, *The Golf Swing* (1974)
32. Murphy, *Golf in the Kingdom* (1972)
33. Nelson, *Shape Your Swing the Modern Way* (1976)
34. Nicklaus, *Golf My Way* (1974)
35. Nicklaus, *My 55 Ways to Lower Your Golf Score* (1964)
36. Nielsen and Beard, *Bad Golf My Way* (1996)_
37. O'Connor, *The Feeling of Greatness* (1995)
38. Owen, *My Usual Game* (1995)
39. Palmer, *The Arnold Palmer Method* (1968)_
40. Pavin, *Corey Pavin's Shotmaking* (1996)
41. Penick, *For All Who Love the Game* (1995)
42. Penick, *Harvey Penick's Little Red Book* (1992)
43. Pipkin, *Fast Greens* (1994)
44. Player, *Gary Player's Golf Secrets* (1962)
45. Price, Charles (Ed.), *The American Golfer* (1964)
46. Price, Nick, *The Swing* (1997)
47. Rankin, *A Woman's Guide to Better Golf* (1995)
48. Rushin, *Road Swing* (1998)
49. Rice and Briggs, *The Duffer's Handbook of Golf* (1926)
50. Sampson, *The Eternal Summer* (1992)
51. Sarazen, *Thirty Years of Championship Golf* (1950)
52. Shackleford, *The Good Doctor Returns* (1998)
53. Shanley, *Fathers, Sons & Golf* (1997)
54. Shay, *40 Common Errors in Golf and How to Correct Them*
55. Sinnette, *Forbidden Fairways* (1998)
56. Smith, *Hit Your Second Shot FIRST* (1999)
57. Smith and Holms, *The Gods of Golf* (1996)
58. Snead and Stump, *The Education of a Golfer* (1962)
59. Snead and Tarde, *Pigeons, Marks, Hustlers and Other Golf Bettors You Can Beat* (1986)_
60. Venturi, *The Venturi Analysis* (1981)
61. Vold, *Different Strokes* (1999)
62. Waggoner, *Divots, Shanks, Gimmes, Mulligans and Chili Dips: A Life in 18 Holes* (1993)
63. Watson, *Getting Up and Down* (1983)
64. Wind, *The Story of American Golf* (1975)
65. Wind and Macdonald (Ed.), *Vardon On Golf* (1989)
66. Wright, *Play Golf the Wright Way* (1962)

Periodicals
1. *Esquire*

2. *Golf Digest*
3. *Golf Illustrated*
4. *Golf for Women*
5. *Golf Magazine*
6. *PGA Tour Partners*
7. *Sky*
8. *Spirit*
9. *Washington Golf Monthly*

And
1. The World Wide Web

Happy Golfing!

Appendix

"Hello, I must be going."
—Captain Geoffrey T. Spaulding

Donald's Book of Lists **Trivia Quiz**
It's time for the Final Exam. Let's see if you were a conscientious reader.

1. Why did they call George Knudson "the maestro?"
2. When did Arnold Palmer win his 14th SPGA tournament?
3. Who is Tiger Woods?
4. What is the difference between "the Grand Slam" and "the Venerable Slam?"
5. Who is a greater golfer: Moe Norman, Greg Norman or Norman Schwarzkopf?
6. Where is the lifeguard station at Pebble Beach?
7. How many ways can a golf ball enter the hole?
8. Juneau the capital of Alaska?

Farewell and Happy Golfing!